Osprey Modelling • 25

Modelling the Mitsubishi A6M Zero

Brian Criner

Consultant editor Robert Oehler • *Series editors* Marcus Cowper and Nikolai Bogdanovic

First published in Great Britain in 2006 by Osprey Publishing
Midland House, West Way, Botley, Oxford OX2 0PH, UK
443 Park Avenue South, New York, NY 10016, USA
Email: info@ospreypublishing.com

ISBN-10: 1-84176-866-9
ISBN-13: 978-1-84176-866-3

Page layout by Servis Filmsetting Ltd, Manchester, UK
Typeset in Monotype Gill Sans and ITC Stone Serif
Index by Alison Worthington
Originated by United Graphics Pte Ltd, Singapore
Printed and bound in China through Bookbuilders

06 07 08 09 10   10 9 8 7 6 5 4 3 2 1

A CIP catalogue record for this book is available from the British Library.

FOR A CATALOGUE OF ALL BOOKS PUBLISHED BY OSPREY MILITARY
AND AVIATION PLEASE CONTACT:

NORTH AMERICA
Osprey Direct, c/o Random House Distribution Center, 400 Hahn Road, Westminster,
MD 21157, USA
E-mail: info@ospreydirect.com

ALL OTHER REGIONS
Osprey Direct UK, P.O. Box 140 Wellingborough, Northants, NN8 2FA, UK
E-mail: info@ospreydirect.co.uk

www.ospreypublishing.com

Photographic credits

The photographs that appear in this work were taken by the
author, with the following indicated exceptions:
DB   Derek Brown (www.buffiesbest.com)
GC   Gregg Cooper
TD   Thierry Dekker

Acknowledgements

First, I want to thank my editors Marcus Cowper and Nikolai
Bogdanovic for their infinite patience. Thanks also go to Bob
Oehler; Karl Madcharo and Steve Monroe; Steve Kays; Gary from
the Military shop; Mike Laxton; Gregg Cooper; Dave Kovak and
Dennis Gerber; Tom from Colpar Hobbies in Aurora, Co.; John
Quint; Marcus Nichols; Derek Brown; Harrison Bull; my children,
Andrew, Lauren and Daniel, for being patient with me and my
hobby; Stan Spooner; Thierry Dekker; Brett Green; John from
White Ensign Models; Fred Medel from Tamiya America; Ryan
Toews; Greg Springer; Jim Long; Taizo Nakamura; Kenji Miyazaki;
David Aiken; Larry and Stan from Evergreen Aviation Museum and
Vintage Aircraft Ltd. in Ft Collins, Co; and Tom Sawyer. The Zero
Colour Matrix Chart was compiled with the help of Ryan Toews,
Greg Springer, and Derek Brown.

Contents

Introduction

The goal or objective of this book is to demonstrate a variety of techniques intended to enhance your Zero modelling. It is not intended as an authoritative resource on the Zero. For anyone interested in historical accuracy when building the Zero (or any other Japanese aircraft type), I recommend the www.J-aircraft.com web site. Ryan Toews, Greg Springer, James Lansdale, Jim Long and David Aiken, among others, are all much more knowledgeable concerning Zero accuracy than I could ever hope to be. They can easily be contacted through the message boards, and most will respond promptly to any question you might have. There will be, no doubt, many mistakes of accuracy in this book – for which I apologize in advance. Unfortunately, some subjects, such as the Zero, remain enigmatic to modellers and history enthusiasts. Almost all examples of this beautiful, elegant aircraft were destroyed at the end of the war, as were most references, engineering diagrams and plans. Much of the information available on this plane has been only recently uncovered.

Both a love for history and a love of art brought me to this hobby. But the love of art came first. So, I try to make sure I have satisfactorily investigated my subject before starting to build. I have seen people fuss over the details of a single build for years; I respect the love of detail and the skill of these people. However, I encourage all model junkies out there to occasionally do a quick, out of the box build. You will be amazed at how satisfying it can be to simply build and paint a model without re-engineering the thing. I see this as a hobby; when it becomes a burden due to the need to satisfy the expectations of others, then it is time to sell off the stockpile of kits and find something new to do.

Modelling is an art form. Like any form of art, motivation comes from inspiration. Art is not regulated by rules; that is, the objective of art is to please the artist, not necessarily the observer. Unfortunately, because of a plethora of 'experts' some modellers today feel the need to model to a particular standard. Many modellers feel bound to the consensus opinion on accuracy or painting or weathering. Personally, I don't think people should feel compelled to make their model 100 per cent authentic. I think most people are satisfied with a model that looks and sits right. Out of the box building, or 'assembling' as some modellers have called it, is often condescended to. Realistically, not all modellers have the time, patience or interest necessary to 'scratchbuild' their subject. Ultimately what keeps an artist interested in their subject is how the subject looks to them. Of course, our hobby does have the obvious connection to history and there ought to be some constraint between ones whims and reality. In the end, an artist must be able to look at their artwork and find some intrinsic beauty in what they have created. I believe the two goals, accuracy and appeal, can and do intersect.

Historical overview of the A6M Zero-sen

The A6M *Rei Shiki Sento Ki*, or *Rei-sen* (meaning Type Zero fighter, or, Zero) was an aircraft that, according to some accounts, had near mythical performance qualities. The aircraft was a result of a request by the Imperial Japanese Navy for a low-wing monoplane with superior speed, range, climb and manoeuvrability. The aircraft performed so well, the military leadership in Japan insisted on its use in combat before performance trials had been completed. The aircraft thus began its long and distinguished career as fighter cover for bombers attacking Chungking in August of 1940. Though the aircraft met no enemy in the skies that day, the pilots of the fighter were ecstatic about their new mount. Not until the fourth mission was the aircraft truly tested though. On September 13,

OPPOSITE **Thierry Dekker's profiles of four Zero variants. (TD)**

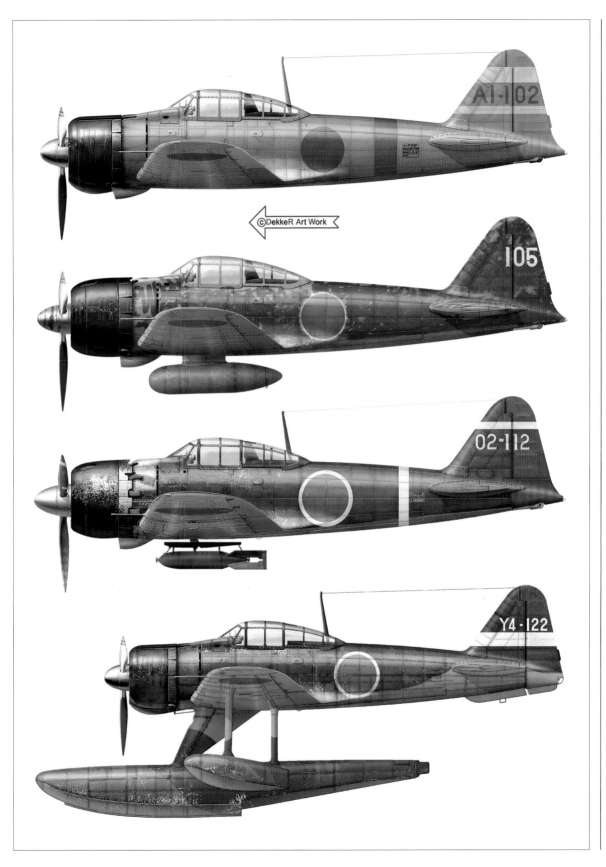

©DekkeR Art Work

during another bomber escort mission to Chungking, the Zero finally met the enemy. In the end, the Zero, without a single loss, shot down 27 Russian-made I-16s. Further embellishment of the Zero legend came from an American observer in China, Claire Chenault, leader of the famous 'Flying Tigers'. He was so impressed with the new type that he sent off urgent messages to Washington, warning them of the abilities of the new fighter. Washington largely wrote off Chenault's warnings as hysteria and exaggeration, but was proven wrong in a most embarrassing way on December 7, 1941, when the Japanese Navy sent waves of bombers and torpedo planes escorted by Zeros to attack Pearl Harbor. Interestingly, it is likely that the superior performance of the Zero heavily influenced Japan's decision to go ahead with the attack on Pearl Harbor.

During the course of the war, the Zero proved itself to be a versatile and deadly adversary. None of the early Allied fighters could match the combat performance of the Zero. There is even a story of some Spitfire pilots that had been transferred from the ETO being given the warning 'never attempt to turn with a Zero'. The pilots, over-confident in regard to the abilities of their aircraft, chose to ignore this advice and were decimated. Eventually, the Allies learned their lesson. With the development of newer, more powerful fighter types by the US and Britain, as well as new tactics that negated the Zero's strengths, the Zero began to show its age. Engineers tried to improve the speed and performance of the Zero by redesigning the wings and fuselage, and by selecting newer, more powerful engines. Designers also recognized the importance of improving the Zero's and the pilot's survivability by adding armour to the plane. However, the increased weight reduced its overall performance. In the end, the Zero was fodder for the waves of American fighter planes swarming over Japan, though in the hands of a skilled, experienced pilot (which was rare by war's end) it was still lethal. Ultimately, with Japan facing certain defeat, the final solution selected by the Japanese military leadership to defend their honour and stave off final defeat involved the use of suicide tactics. Throughout the kamikaze campaign at the end of the war, the Zero was the most common aircraft type used.

Only a few airworthy examples of the Zero remain, and of these only the A6M5 owned by the Planes of Fame museum in Chino, California possesses an authentic Sakai radial engine.[1]

---

1 This will change with the completion of the A6M3 being built by Vintage Aircraft Ltd./Evergreen Aviation Museum in Ft Collins, Colorado.

Tools of the modeller

Having the right tools can instantly make your models better, and the ones that I consider essential are listed below.

Airbrush choice will make a dramatic difference in the quality of a paint job. More important, though, is the painter's willingness to practise. Learning how to use your airbrush, knowing its strengths and weak points, will help you avoid time-consuming mistakes. I prefer double-action airbrushes because I like to be able to instantly control the mixture of air and paint. I know a number of outstanding modellers that prefer single-action airbrushes. The Paasche VL is what I have always used for my airbrushing. Iwata, Badger, Testors and Tamiya all make excellent airbrushes, though the differences in price can be wide. Consider your purchase of this tool carefully. You may save money buying a cheaper airbrush, but your final result can be dramatically different depending on the kind selected.

You can spend a lot or a little on a **compressor**. Simple household compressors (I call them 'bike tyre compressors') are easily found at local hardware stores; they are relatively inexpensive and are fairly durable. They are also loud. Choose your compressor carefully. If you get one without a tank, not only will you eventually go deaf, you will probably burn it out from overuse in a relatively short time. I use an Iwata compressor purchased from a friend. They are expensive, but when they click on, they won't disturb your concentration or interrupt conversation.

I avoided buying an **Etchmate** for years – what a mistake! There are several different types available on the market. I use the one from Mission Models. These tools are irreplaceable when it comes to manipulating photoetch.

I have seen a few discussions related to the value of a **Dremel tool with Flexi-shaft extension**. They are handy little tools and I am amazed that some people fail to find them useful. I use this tool for cutting tubing, for grinding down pieces I want to modify, for drilling, and for polishing. I consider it a must-have tool.

A **magnifier** is essential for looking at tiny pieces. This tool will help you keep your eyesight and your sanity. I use a magnifying lamp mounted on a moveable arm. These are common items at stores with a large lighting section.

Other essential tools for the modeller include **hemostats/fine scissors, files, sticky labels** (for staying organized), and a **pin vice** (with spare drill bits).

A6M2-N Rufe (1/48)

Subject:	A6M2-N Rufe
Modeller/photos:	Brian Criner
Skill level	Intermediate
Base kit:	Hasegawa
Scale:	1/48
Additional detailing sets used:	Eduard Coloured seat belts
Decals:	From kit
Paints:	White Ensign's Nakajima Interior Green, Mitsubishi Navy Green
	Testors Model Master Rust, Italian Red, Buffable Aluminum
	Grumbacher Burnt Umber

The A6M2-N Rufe was a formidable foe for Allied fighters early in the war. It was an aircraft with excellent performance despite its bulky floats. Surprisingly, there is relatively little in the way of photo references showing Rufes in frontline service. Most photos are grainy, and fail to satisfactorily show the type of wear pattern characteristic of a plane subjected to the weathering of the sea. I was able to piece together enough information about typical wear by looking at the photos available and basically inferring what I couldn't see.

One particularly interesting characteristic of Rufes was that they were initially painted in the offensive *Tsuchi-Iro* scheme. Later, in the field, Rufes were over-coated in the defensive 'topside' green. In addition, all or almost all Zeros were primed with a red-oxide primer right up to the end of the war. First, this means the existence of a 'chipped up' Zero with large sections of natural metal showing would have been unusual to say the least. Exposure of natural metal, if present, would more likely have been in the form of scuffmarks, not peeled paint. My goal was to keep 'chipping' to a minimum, yet still show the intense wear these aircraft experienced. So I needed to figure out how to wear away the paint in a subtle manner that gradually exposed all the layers of colour, from natural metal through the primer and *Tsuchi-Iro* to the topside green defensive paint. The final model shows more 'chipping' than I had planned due to a masking error, of which more later. Since the focus of this project was the exterior finish, little was done to modify the kit other than the addition of a resin seat from CMK, coloured seatbelts from Eduard, and some other bits and pieces.

Cockpit and engine

The cockpit was painted in White Ensign Models (WEM) Nakajima Interior Green. The sidewalls from Hasegawa, quite basic in detail, were brought to life with dry-brushing and highlight painting. A wash of artist oils finished off the interior. For the instrument panel, I used the kit-provided decals for the instrument faces. After numerous applications of MicroSol, the dial faces, cut out with a Squadron Punch and Die set, sank down into their recesses. To accentuate the glass dial, each face received a drop of Future Floor Wax.

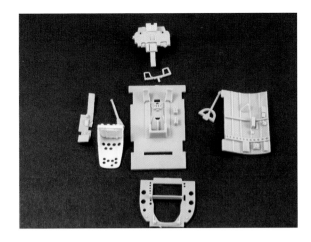

For this project the kit cockpit was used. Only the seat was replaced (using the excellent CMK example).

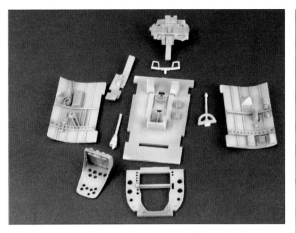

The cockpit was sprayed with White Ensign's Nakajima Interior Green. The colour cup was lightened with a drop each of Beige and White and then highlighted. The purpose is to create the feel of depth.

Since this build was primarily 'out of the box', I decided to restrict the engine detailing to painting. Cylinders and crankcase were painted silver and a wash of Burnt Umber artist oil tinted with black was added.

Assembly

One of my concerns building this model was to add enough weight to the float of the Rufe to get it to sit correctly in its docking cradle. I used lead pellets (from a pellet gun) and a lead fishing sinker hammered to shape. All this was held in place with superglue (cyanoacrylate, or CA). After the fuselage was mated and wings attached I added the float, making sure to align it longitudinally with the axis of the fuselage. All seams were filled with superglue, sanded with 320- through 800-grit wet-dry sandpaper. When using the more coarse grits, I masked panel lines and any other surface features I wanted to protect with Tamiya tape.

The cockpit components after painting. Despite lacking aftermarket offerings, the cockpit looks great when put together.

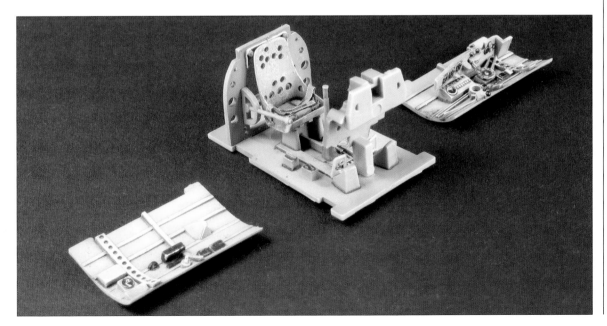

The 'lack' of detail in the cockpit components will be barely visible in the finished model.

Paint preparations

Since my focus in this build was on the finish, I made sure the surface of the model was perfect before painting. All panel lines were inspected to ensure there were no interruptions due to sanding or assembly. Lost panel lines were replaced with a scribing tool or an X-acto blade. A panel line repair typically missed after sanding is the wing leading edge, so extra attention was given to this area. After all repairs were made, the entire model was polished with fine-grit steel wool. This is a great tool for getting into hard-to-reach areas like the wing to fuselage join at the wing leading edge. Steel wool conforms nicely to the compound curves of the fuselage and wing without creating sanding lines or ruining the camber of the wing. Once the entire model looked smooth and relatively scratch free, it was polished with a polishing wheel in my Dremel. This can be a daunting process for obvious reasons, but I use only the laminated cotton-polishing disc, not the felt disc. When polishing, I am always mindful of the direction of rotation of the wheel (clockwise from the user's perspective), so that edges and corners are always polished with the wheel rotating from the model surface toward the edge. Violating this credo can result in your model being tossed across the room. As long as care is taken with the amount of pressure applied, burning the plastic is not an issue. This is something that takes a bit practice to feel comfortable with.

Painting layers

Because the model has so many layers of paint, it is important to keep your paint well thinned. I sprayed each layer with about 40 parts pigment to 60 parts thinner. The model was first sprayed with several coats of Testors Model Master Buffable Aluminum. About 15 minutes after each coat, the paint was polished to a shine with a Dremel wheel. Next, the silver was given a protective coat of Future Floor Wax. Once this was dry (c.30–40 minutes) the entire model was sprayed with Red-Oxide red. To obtain this colour, I used Testors Model Master 'Rust', which is just a bit too brown, tinted red with a few drops of Testors Italian Red. I wanted this layer to look as much as possible like the rusty red paint showing on the wing of the A6M3 at Vintage Aircraft Ltd. in Ft Collins. Next, the model was sprayed *Tsuchi-Iro* using the mix of Testors enamels decribed in detail on page 34. The model was then pre-shaded with Testors Burnt Umber, after which the model received a coat of White Ensign's IJN Green. When spraying over the pre-shading, I tried to cover the pre-shading to the point where it showed through the topside green, but not so much that it was obvious.

The next step in the painting process is post-shading. The goal here is to give the finish dimension, not create an effect that didn't exist on the real aircraft. If the pre-shading and post-shading are too stark, they become too noticeable. To post-shade, I add a drop or two of a lighter colour, usually Testors MM Flat White, Ivory or Sand to the cup. In this case I used Testors Sand to lighten the topside green. The mix must be very thin. Test-spraying on a piece of white paper is essential. The paint must spray in a feathered pattern with absolutely no speckling (the latter means the paint is too thick). I paint where light can be seen reflecting off the model as I spray, to ensure I do not go too far; it's important for me to see the paint actually hitting the surface. I want the colour difference to be almost imperceptible, which means a minimum amount of paint. In all of the vintage photographs I have seen of operational World War II aircraft, the surface paint possesses an almost infinite range of hues and

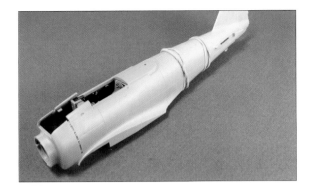

Once the fuselage halves were together, I began work on the float. It is important to add considerable weight to the float if you want the model to sit properly in its cradle when complete. I started with a piece of lead fishing sinker, hammered to shape on a concrete floor, and then added small lead pellets that had also been hammered flat to save on space. With the addition of a few blobs of superglue I was ready to glue the halves together.

Once all the main assemblies were constructed I dry-fitted the parts to see if the plane would stay on its nose.

Attention to detail is essential in getting the right finish. After re-scribing any lost panel lines and filling any seams that needed this doing, I began the 'smoothing' process. I do not put paint on the plane until I have a mirror-like finish on the plastic. Although this is admittedly a bit of overkill, it ensures the finish will be free of defects. This is especially important if your model will have a natural metal finish. I start by using fine-grade steel wool.

Once the model is relatively smooth, I finish by polishing the entire model with a polishing wheel mounted on a Dremel tool. Be sure to use the stitched, laminated cotton disc and not the 'felt' disc. This process will leave your model with a glass-like finish.

Because some metal surfaces will be showing after the weathering process, the entire model is painted with a couple of coats of Testors Model Master Metalizer. Though only a few spots will be showing through, I've found it's easier to coat the entire model with the silver paint in order to avoid 'chipping' through to grey plastic.

It is essential that the model be coated *after* the spraying of silver with a complete coat of Future Floor wax. Otherwise the weathering process will wear the paint down to the grey plastic.

Next, the model is painted in Red-Oxide primer. This primer was commonly used on Japanese naval aircraft, and on Zeros in particular. The primer worked so well, it is still visible on the wing of this decaying A6M3.

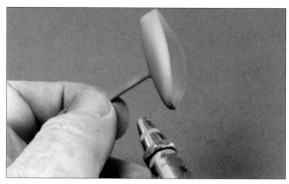

The primer was recreated by starting with a thinned paint cup of Testors Rust. In order to tint the paint to more of a red, I added a few drops of Testors Italian Red to the cup. This mix was then sprayed over the silver.

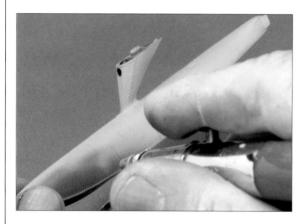

Next, Grey Green was sprayed over the primer. The original Rufes sent into the war were painted overall *Tsuchi-Iro*. As the war progressed, and the hunters became the hunted, most Rufes were field-painted with the defensive green topcoat over the top of the original *Tsuchi-Iro*.

It is important at this stage that the paint completely covers the base coat, but is still kept thin. Since several coats of paint are going to be on this bird, surface details will begin to disappear if the coats are too thick.

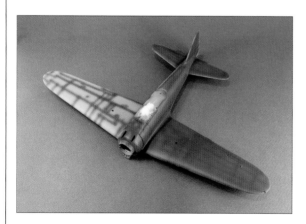

After painting the *Tsuchi-Iro*, the model was pre-shaded with Burnt Umber and then coated with White Ensign's IJN Green.

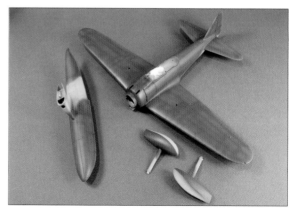

The green was tinted by post-shading with lightened colours of the base coat.

contrasts caused by staining from weather, refuelling, the feet of ground crew, the replacement of panels, or repainting.

Weathering

My goal was to weather the paint so that each layer was visible without having to peel or heavily chip it, which would be inappropriate for a primed aircraft. I wanted to show a gradual, almost feathered gradation between layers that would reflect the wear and tear consistent with an aircraft in constant use in rough conditions. I considered using the paint-and-pull technique, in which masking tape is used to pull layers of paint up. However, using this technique would pull through all the layers of paint, giving a 'peeled' look to the finish. Another approach I considered involved using salt, or white glue placed in spots between the layers of paint. This is later pulled or rubbed off, exposing the layers beneath. Again, the 'patchy' effect created by this technique was not what I was looking for. A friend of mine suggested I use the Paasche Air Eraser. This tool shoots a very fine grade 'dust', actually microscopic beads, to erode the surface of the model. My friend tried this technique to create a gradual, wearing away of the paint. Although this effect looked amazing on my friend's model, I thought it looked a bit 'pebbly' or grainy. I wanted to create an almost imperceptible weathering of the paint. I realized I was going to have to figure out a new technique for creating this effect.

Initially, I practised with fine-grade steel wool. This did create a finer 'wear pattern', but left scratches that looked unrealistic to me. I decided to try plastic polishing compound. I had some McGuire's fine grade polishing compound (Blue Magic also makes a suitable product) that I used to polish canopies. I placed a small amount of compound on a slightly moistened Q-tip (or cotton bud) and gently rubbed the surface of the paint. To my surprise, this allowed me to wear away the paint gradually, layer by layer. The key to making this work is to keep the amount of compound used minimal. Your applicator, or whatever is used to manipulate the compound, should have a fairly narrow diameter. I actually used sprue cutters to cut the top of the Q-tip down by half, giving me better resolution. Once I had created a pattern that I was pleased with, I decided to add a few small chips. I wanted to keep the chips to a minimum, as I didn't want to detract from the effect created by the polishing compound. To create these chips I used a micro-dissection scalpel with a curved tip to 'pick' at the surface until I had exposed a small amount of silver. As always, it is prudent to keep your weathering to a minimum. It's easier to add more weathering later than to remove excess. So go slow and stop often, and only add a little at a time.

The next step in the weathering process involved spraying a layer of 'flat' and then a wash of Burnt Umber. The wash was wiped off until very little residue showed on the Q-tip. When I was satisfied the residue wash had been removed, I shot the model with another coat of Clear Flat. This was necessary because the process of wiping the wash from the surface will wear through the flat coat, creating a 'patchy' appearance where the undercoat of Future is showing through. To finish off the weathering, I used a chrome Berol pencil to add fine chips in spots where there was no undercoat. Next, I streaked the surface of the model with some Desert Sand MIG pigment on a flat chisel-tip brush. Wiping the model with a Q-tip, following the same direction as the brush, followed this. This removed the excess pigment, leaving a hint of the MIG pigments behind. The floats received similar treatment. I used tiny spots of artist oils and pulled them down, top to bottom, instead of pulling the pigment back as was done on the wing and fuselage surfaces.

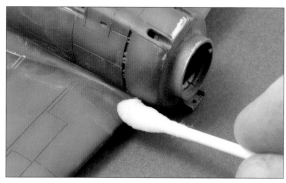

In order to wear gradually through the surface paint, I chose to use fine-grade plastic polishing compound. The brand I used was McGuire's, but there are several on the market that would no doubt give identical results.

To make this technique work properly, start with a moistened Q-tip. Use a very small amount of compound. Work the compound in gently until you are barely able to see the underside colours coming through. To reduce the amount of Q-tip in contact with the model (and thereby increase control over how much paint was removed) I clipped the end of the Q-tip with a pair of sprue cutters.

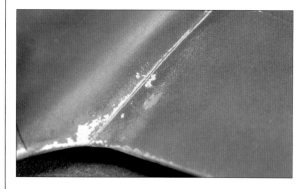

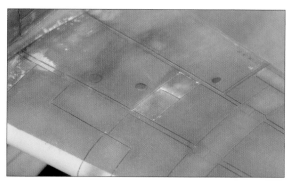

In order to simulate more obvious wear and tear I used a micro dissection scalpel. Gentle and careful chipping accentuates the subtle wear from the polishing compound. The abrasion was applied to areas of the aircraft that were likely to see constant wear and tear, such as the wing roots and the floats.

After application of the polishing compound, the overall surface was again coated with Future. The surface of the model was then washed liberally with Grumbacher's Burnt Umber artist oils thinned with Turpenoid.

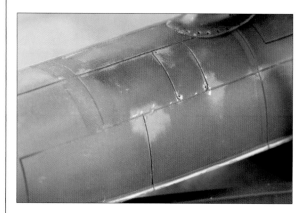

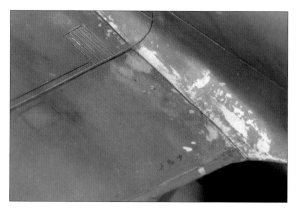

MIG pigments and thin washes of artist oil pigment were used to create stains resulting from refuelling and maintenance by the ground crews.

The weathering process did cause some minor damage to a few of the decals. As long as the damage is minimal, it can be considered authentic wear and tear. Some minor chipping with the dissection scalpel was also executed .

The kit engine was used out of the box. It was painted Aluminum, coated with Future Floor Wax and then given a wash of Burnt Umber oil paint.

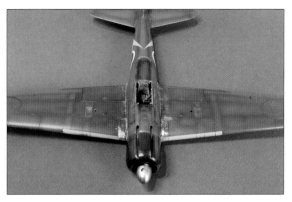

After weathering and the addition of the engine, the cowl and spinner were painted and added. Since the Rufe was a Nakajima product, the cowl should be black rather than blue-black. The spinner was painted with Buffable Aluminum and then polished with the Dremel tool.

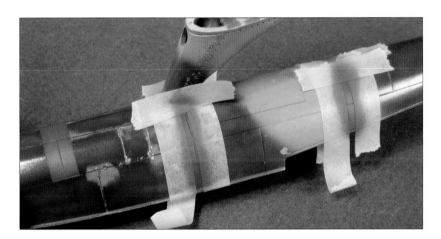

The markings for the float were masked with Tamiya tape and painted with Testors Italian Red. After the float had been weathered, the markings were weathered in a manner similar to the rest of the aircraft.

A shot just prior to the final weathering aircraft. The decals are the kit-supplied ones, which settled nicely into seams after some coaxing with MicroSol. A frustrating reality with the Hasegawa Rufe is that several decals, including the tail markings, were slightly out of register.

Small drops of various tones of brown pigment were placed randomly into several panel lines on the float and then the pigment was drawn down with vertical strokes of a clean, dry brush. The technique was repeated on the wings and on certain parts of the fuselage.

The boarding ladder was slightly weathered with the addition of some metal chipping with a Berol pencil. The tie-down hook on the tail is moulded into the kit, but appeared too thick and was subsequently replaced with fine wire bent to shape.

Various panels were accentuated by post-shading with lightened versions of the base coat, or very thin mixes of tans and browns. The wing ID strips should be painted before adding the silver, rust, greens etc. Masking these panels without pulling the paint from below is just tedious. As can be seen in this photo, I was not completely successful when removing the tape.

Gun barrels were replicated using fine-gauge Minimeca tubing. The bombs were provided in the kit. The fuel line running from the front of the float to the engine bottom is provided as a thick plastic blob in the kit. It was replaced with thin metal wire bent to shape.

The Rufe experienced some pretty harsh environmental conditions where it served in the Pacific. Proper weathering, if done modestly, really gives the aircraft character.

Additional weathering was added with a Berol chrome coloured pencil to wing-walk areas and high-use areas around the cockpit. In order to get the best use out of the pencil, make sure your tips are as sharp as you can get them. In order to extend the life of your pencil, sharpen it on a piece of coarse sandpaper rather than using a pencil sharpener.

Kamikaze A6M5c (1/72)

Subject:	A6M5c kamikaze
Modeller/photos:	Brian Criner
Skill level:	Intermediate
Base kit:	Hasegawa A6M5c
Scale:	1/72
Additional detailing sets used:	True Details resin wheels, Eduard coloured seat belts, Aires resin interior, bomb from Fujimi C6M kit, Evergreen plastic sheet and rod Fine-gauge solder Fine-gauge copper wire Fine-gauge steel wire Minimeca tubing
Decals:	From kit
Paints:	Testors Model Master Enamels: SAC Bomber Tan; Flat White; Flat Black; Zinc Chromate, Ivory. White Ensign Enamels: Mitsubishi Cowl Blue-Black; Mitsubishi Interior Green; Mitsubishi Naval Green. Tamiya Acrylics: Clear Blue, Red, Green.

Although I mostly stick to 1/48 scale, after inspecting and photographing Derek Brown's work on an A6M2 my interest in 1/72 was rekindled. Hasegawa's line of 1/72-scale A6Ms are as well done as their 1/48-scale series. On this project, I wanted to represent a loaded-up Zero, destined to become a kamikaze. Aircraft used as suicide bombers were initially outdated fighters, such as the A6M2. Frontline fighters such as the A6M5c usually acted as escorts, engaging and distracting the combat air patrols of the US Navy. Eventually, when successes of the special attack squadrons became better known, and when all other forms of

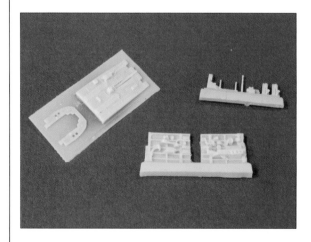

The very nice Aires resin set for the Hasegawa kit. Unfortunately, my sample contained a 1/35-scale tank commander's head instead of a seat. So I used the kit seat out of necessity.

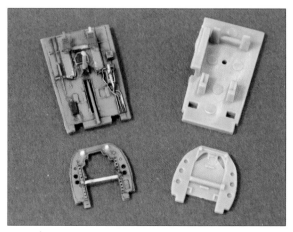

The Aires set makes a big difference to the appearance of the cockpit.

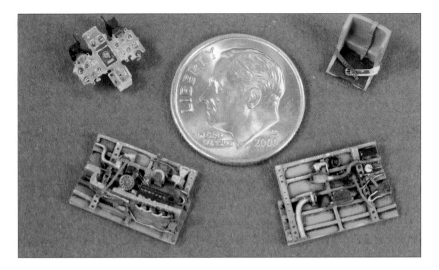

The resin sidewalls are nicely done but need to be thinned down to the point of near transparency in order to fit in the tight quarters of the cockpit. The kit seat is not to scale and should be thinned down if used. Eduard coloured belts were added to the seat.

attack had been neutralized by Allied air superiority, any aircraft that could carry bombs was used as a suicide plane.

I wanted this subject to look weathered, as if it had been regularly used or had been sitting on an airstrip somewhere ready for action. Because this aircraft was an A6M5c, a later model of the Zero with a new gun configuration, weathering of the wing surfaces would not be too extensive. I also needed a 1/72-scale bomb, since one was not provided with the kit. I found a bomb and rack in a Fujimi C6M Myrt kit.

The canopy of the Hasegawa kit comes closed, but since I planned on using the very nice Aires interior I needed to figure out how to open up the one-piece canopy provided with the model, preferably with a minimum of work and a minimum of clean up. My options were: 1 – vacuform a new canopy; 2 – obtain a Squadron canopy; or 3 – modify the existing canopy. I chose option 3. Since opening the kit canopy destroys one of the three parts at the expense of the other two, I needed another canopy. I got the second canopy from an A6M3 kit, also from Hasegawa. Once I had all of the pieces cleaned up and polished, they were masked and painted. I wanted to open the flaps up, but with no aftermarket parts obtainable in my time frame, I decided to scratchbuild them.

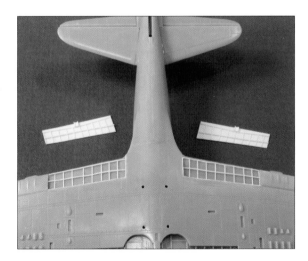

I wanted to show the flaps deployed, so it was necessary to cut the flaps out of the wings and replace them with new ones made from Evergreen sheet and strip styrene.

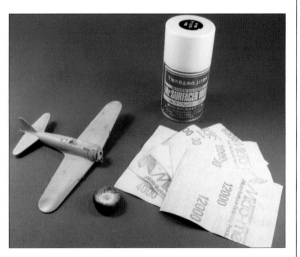

Micro-mesh polishing cloth and Dremel polishing discs were used to achieve a smooth finish before painting. After a nice sheen is achieved, Mr. Surfacer 1000 is applied to fill in any scratches.

Cockpit

Aires makes a great little cockpit specifically for the A6M5. Unfortunately mine contained a 1/35-scale tank commander's head in place of the seat! This made it necessary to modify the kit seat. I did this by filing down the seat sides, which are way oversize in scale (in retrospect, I should have taken the sides down even more as they are still too thick). The seat was highlighted with coloured photoetch seatbelts from Eduard. The resin pieces provided by Aires (including the head) are nicely detailed and really add to the kit. The sidewall pieces were quite thick and required thinning of the backing with sandpaper. Once again, I stopped short of the appropriate thickness, and I ended up with fit problems when the fuselage sides came together. After some fidgeting around, I was able to get all of the interior pieces together. A frustrating point with the Aires set was the lack of a good positive fit for the instrument panel. Quite a few adjustments were necessary before the panel was positioned appropriately. Behind the seat, the adjustment bungee was recreated with stretched sprue. Side panel and floor construction went smoothly, with no modifications other than the resin and photoetch supplied by the Aires set.

Engine

Since I had skimped on the engine detailing in my first build, I decided I would redeem myself by wiring up the engine. The wiring for each cylinder was replicated by drilling the front and back of each cylinder with my smallest drill bit. My source for wire was stereo speaker wire stripped of its insulation. The tiny little threads were then pulled from the main wire. Cylinder head supports were made from narrow-gauge steel wire. The box atop the crankcase was a piece of styrene block cut to size. Be careful when attaching the engine to the fuselage.

Flaps

Flaps were constructed from .010 sheet styrene. I carefully cut them out of the wings and used them as templates to construct the new styrene flaps. Panel lines were measured out and drawn in with pencil. I then made gentle strokes with a scribing tool held true by a straight edge. Individual ribs were cut to size from styrene strip and an X-acto blade, and glued in place with Tamiya liquid cement. Actuators on the bottom flap were made from Evergreen I-beam, shaped with an X-acto blade. The lower flaps were left off until construction and painting were finished.

Painting

Once the fuselage was buttoned up, and the seams filled, the entire aircraft was sanded and polished using 3,200–12,000 polishing cloths. I wanted to be certain the finish was perfectly smooth before painting. Next I primed all exterior surfaces with Mr. Surfacer 1000 and then polished the surface again, this time using a Dremel/polishing wheel combination. The surface of the model was then pre-shaded with Burnt Umber and then painted with the surface colours (WEM's Mitsubishi Navy Green on top and a slightly lightened mix of *Tsuchi-Iro*). I then lighted the surface colours slightly with just a couple of drops of Testors Ivory in the paint cup. Next I lightened the mix just a bit more and redid the control surfaces (those on top). Wing tips and leading edge ID bands were masked with Tamiya tape and sprayed. The cowl was sprayed with WEM Mitsubishi Cowl Blue-Black. The perimeter around the flaps and wheel wells was masked and sprayed with my *aotake* mix (see the *Colour Reference Chart*, item 8). A coat of Future preceded the application of decals. All of the exhaust stacks come separate on the Hasegawa kit except for the bottom pair; they were painted with Testors Rust, followed by a coat of Clear Flat. The bottle of Flat I used had most of the clear carrier dumped out, with just the 'cloudy' flat left. This helped in the next step.

After a satisfactory finish was achieved, the entire model was pre-shaded with Burnt Umber.

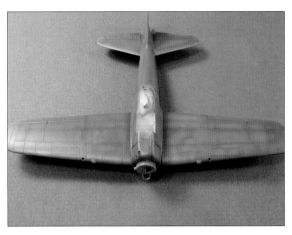

After pre-shading, the model was covered with White Ensign Mitsubishi Navy Green. The lower surface colours were a mix of Model Master SAC Bomber Tan, Zinc Chromate and Flat White.

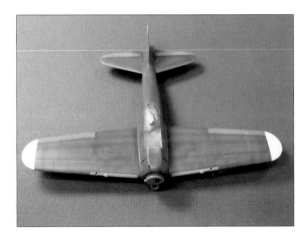

Next, the wing leading edge bands were painted yellow and the wing tips were painted white.

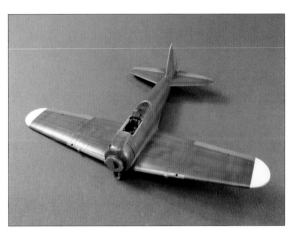

The turtle deck was painted with White Ensign Cowl Blue-Black.

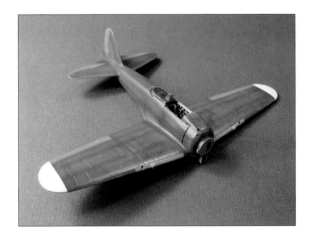

The entire model was then covered with Future Floor Wax.

The holes for the bomb rack needed to be drilled out.

ABOVE The wheel wells and flaps were then painted *aotake*.

ABOVE RIGHT The engine was detailed with copper wire taken from a stereo speaker. The magneto was made from Evergreen stock.

RIGHT The one-piece canopy was cut apart using a razor saw. Two canopies were used to create one. The canopy pieces were then masked with Tamiya tape.

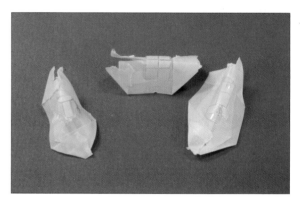

BELOW Once the exhaust stacks were attached, they were painted with Model Master Burnt Iron mixed with Steel. The stacks were then treated with the Rustall system (which comes in four bottles) to achieve the correct finish.

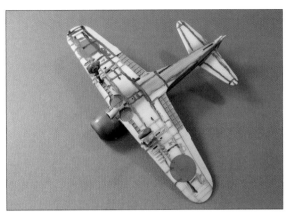

Attaching the engine was a tricky process; take care to ensure the engine lines up properly in the middle of the cowling. The landing gear legs were weak and broke off a couple of times. They were strengthened by drilling out the top of the struts and the wheel well inserts, and adding steel wire.

The model was given a rather thick wash of Burnt Umber.

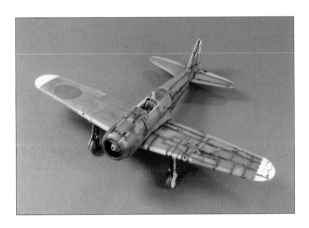

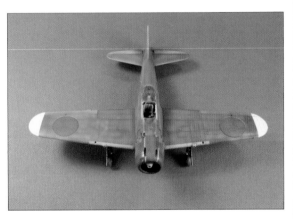

The paint was allowed to dry before removal. This is later removed using a Q-tip moistened in Turpenoid.

After removal of the wash, the leftover pigment in the recesses is just the right amount.

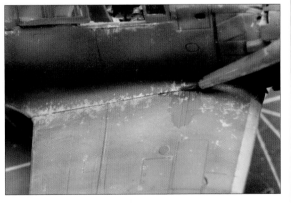

After the pencil chipping, the aircraft was given a coat of Clear Flat to both flatten the silver chipping effect as well as seal the paint. A final thin 'dirt' wash was added to the Flat finish, giving a nice 'stained' look.

Additional weathering and chipping was accomplished with a Berol silver pencil.

ABOVE Certain areas, such as the wing roots, were given an extra wash of Burnt Umber.

ABOVE RIGHT The wash was then wiped out with Q-tips.

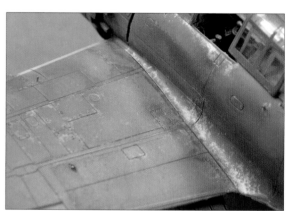

RIGHT A very thin mix of Black, Tan and Clear Flat was used to spray the exhaust stains. This mix also has the effect of muting the bright silver from the silver pencil.

BELOW The antennae wire was created using fine-gauge transparent nylon thread. The decals were weathered by spraying them with a coat of very thin Clear Flat with a single drop of Testors Sand or Beige.

The bomb and rack were constructed using parts obtained from a 1/72-scale Fujimi Myrt kit. The rack was modified to fit the Zero. Stabilizing wires added to the front and rear of the bomb were made of clear nylon thread.

Landing gear

The fit of the landing gear was a bit sloppy. About five minutes after attaching the gear and carefully inspecting the angle of sit, I dropped the plane on the floor! Both gears broke off, as did one of the horizontal tail surfaces. After a bit of cussing and ranting I reattached the gear by drilling a tiny hole in the top of it and one in the wing area where the gear inserted. I then glued a small piece of wire into the top of the gear and glued the gear back into the wings. The tail wheel and boot were painted black. By this stage of the war, few aircraft carried tailhooks. I decided, for the sake of convenience, to leave mine in. The arresting hook was painted black, although Ryan Toews believes there is evidence that they may have been painted *aotake*.

Conclusion

Despite being a tiny kit, the Hasegawa 1/72 Zero can be built into an impressive representation of the Zero with careful painting and weathering. The Aires interior set was outstanding; I'm still not sure what to make of the 1/35-scale tank commander's head though...

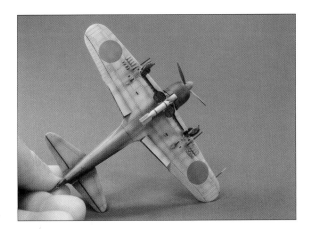

Dirt, grime and exhaust stains were added to the bottom of the aircraft in a fashion similar to the top surfaces. I sprayed a very thin mix of Clear Flat, two drops of Black and a drop of Tan along the bottom surfaces in the direction of airflow. It is also important to note that the tailhook should be faired over, as very few, if any, of the A6M5cs, flew from carriers. The tailhook would have been removed to save weight.

The starboard wing showing the weathering along the wing root to good effect. Be careful with your chipping. Unlike many other Japanese aircraft from the period, Zero surface paint was resilient as it was sprayed over a primed surface right up until the end of the war. I tried to restrict the chipping to the areas of the aircraft that were likely to get a lot of foot traffic.

ABOVE The kit-supplied 20mm gun barrels were not used as they were rather oversized. In their place I used fine-gauge syringe tubing cut to length. I added the flash suppressor portion of the kit guns to the front of the syringe tubing.

BELOW The finished model from the port side.

A6M2 model 21, Pearl Harbor (1/48)

Subject:	*A6M2 model 21, Soryu Air Wing, Pearl Harbor raid*
Modeller:	*Brian Criner*
Skill level:	*Advanced*
Base kit:	*Hasegawa A6M2b-21*
Scale:	*1/48*
Additional detailing sets used:	*True Details resin wheels, Eduard coloured seat belts*
	CMK resin interior
	Cutting Edge ailerons
	Verlinden flaps/rudder/horizontal control surfaces/folding wing tips
	Moskit exhaust stubs
	Evergreen plastic rod
	Fine-gauge solder
	Fine-gauge copper wire
	Fine-gauge steel wire
	Minimeca tubing
	25-gauge syringe needles
Decals:	*From kit*
Paints:	*Model Master Enamels: SAC Bomber Tan; Flat White; Flat Black; Zinc Chromate.*
	White Ensign Enamels: Mitsubishi Cowl Blue/Black; Mitsubishi Interior Green.

There is an abundance of Zero kits available in just about every scale. In my opinion, the Hasegawa 1/48-scale series provides some of the best. Just about every variant of the Zero is represented; detail is crisp and flash free. As is common in Hasegawa kits, the cockpit could benefit from the improvement of aftermarket offerings. The A6M2 variants have no options for dropped flaps. Additionally, there are minor inaccuracies in the representation of cockpit equipment.

Cockpit painting and construction

Starting with the cockpit, I began adding wire to the sidewalls and floorboard. I used lead fishing line as my wiring source. Since it is difficult to represent every wire in the actual cockpit, I endeavoured to represent the detail as thoroughly as possible. The CMK cockpit is a delightful little set, combining resin with photoetch to make perhaps the most accurate aftermarket set for Zeros in this scale. The set comes with pieces to represent an M2, M3 or M5 variant of the Zero. Cockpit sidewalls were further enhanced with levers and handles made from fine-gauge solder and steel wire. Knobs at the ends of the handles were represented, in most cases, by adding a small blob of Kristal Klear to the end of the rod. When dry, the knob can be painted, creating a convincing ball. (If you need to modify the 'ball' at the end of the rod, you must do so before the Kristal Klear gets too dry.) In order to enhance the back of the cockpit, I added styrene strip to represent the fuselage stringers. As nice as this looks initially, the reality is that it is nearly impossible to make out once the fuselage halves are together (but I know it's there!)

Accessories used on the Hasegawa kit include Verlinden photoetch and resin parts (the folding wing tips, rudder and horizontal tail surfaces), Cutting Edge ailerons, and Moskit exhaust stubs.

The excellent CMK update was used for the cockpit. The kit includes parts for all Zero variants.

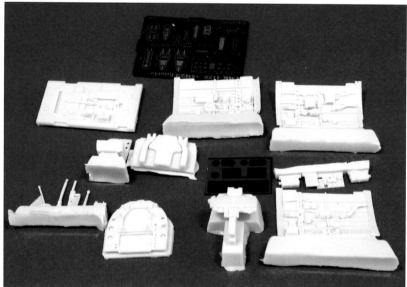

Once the floor and sidewalls were sufficiently modified, I sprayed them Interior Green. I used White Ensigns Mitsubishi Interior Green from their Japanese Aircraft Enamel line. These are wonderful paints that come in small tins similar to the Humbrol offerings. The paints cover nicely, and are, for the most part, fairly accurate. After looking at photos of Tenzo Nakamura's beautiful instrument panel recreations, as well as some other reference photos, I would probably tint this colour a bit to the darker side. The photos I viewed of Mitsubishi interiors show the colour to be a bit darker than WEM's representation. The paint looked remarkably close to American Interior Green. After my initial coat of paint, I add one to two drops of a lighter colour to the cup (Flat White, Light Tan, or Testors Ivory work well). I always test-spray on paper that contrasts with the colour I am using. When highlight painting with a darker or lighter colour than the base, I feel it is essential the paint be very thin (approximately 70 parts thinner to 30 parts

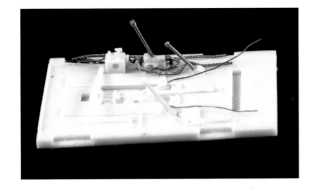

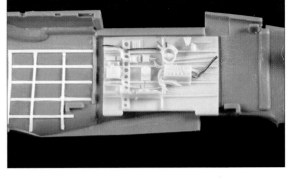

The resin floorboard was spruced up with the addition of lead and copper wire. Handles on the top of the levers were created using the Squadron product Kristal Klear.

The framing behind the bulkhead was detailed with Evergreen styrene. Ultimately, it is difficult to see in the finished model.

paint, although I don't measure it that way; I simply thin until my test-spray is devoid of 'speckles'. I use this lightened spray to highlight panel centres, seat backs and various parts of the floorboard. My intention with highlight painting is to give the perception of depth. Highlight painting is followed by the painting of the various cockpit components. In order to achieve an accurate finish for your Zero, I recommend visiting the web site www.J-aircraft.com. This is your best source (in English anyway), for information on building and painting any Japanese military aircraft from World War II. In particular, the articles by Ryan Toews and Greg Springer are helpful in getting your colours straight.

Once the detail painting is finished, a coat of Future Floor Wax is applied. This protects my enamel finish from the next stage of finishing. When the Future is dry (no longer tacky to the touch), I mix up a broth of Grumbacher oil paint thinned with either Turpenoid or Ronsonal lighter fluid. I usually use the Turpenoid, as it is not as 'hot' and less likely to eat through the Future and attack the paint underneath. Small crevices and corners get a pin wash, which is a small amount of pigment on a 'wet', fine-point brush. Colour of choice for washes is typically Burnt Umber. After removing the excess pigment, I applied a thin coat of Testors Clear Flat. Next, I mixed up some of the base cockpit colour lightened with a couple of drops of white. Using a soft, chisel-tip brush, I dry-brushed the cockpit components to bring out the surface details. Some detailing using Berol Prismacolor pencils follows dry-brushing. These pencils are excellent for pinpoint detailing. Finishing out the cockpit area, I painted the turtle deck behind the pilot's roll bar and the cockpit coaming under the windscreen in with White Ensign's Mitsubishi Cowl Blue-Black.

Engine detailing

I initially chose to use the CMK Sakai engine set for this kit. The engine is beautifully moulded and crisply detailed, especially the crankcase. I carefully assembled the engine, adding bracing struts made from steel wire and was preparing to add the ignition harness and cables when it occurred to me that I had better test-fit the engine before continuing. The engine fitted nicely, but to my frustration was too large in diameter to allow the cowling around it. Apparently, the engine is to be displayed with cowling sitting beside the aircraft, but I had decided before starting this project that I wanted to display the aircraft with the engine enclosed within the cowling. Somewhat frustrated, I proceeded to start over. This time I used the cylinders provided by the kit, adding the CMK crankcase to the front of the kit cylinders. After having spent so much time working on the CMK engine, I decided to add the new engine with few modifications save the crankcase and pushrods. See the Zero Colour Matrix chart on pp.68–70 for details of how to paint your engine.

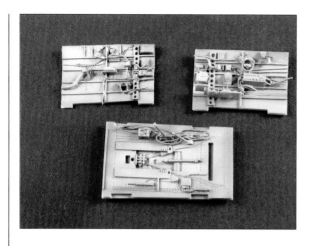

White Ensign's Mitsubishi Interior Green was used to paint the resin parts.

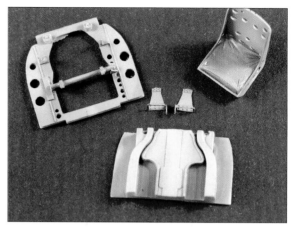

A lightened mixture of the base colours was used to add contrast to the parts.

I decided not to detail the area behind the bulkhead because I figured it would not be very visible in the finished aircraft.

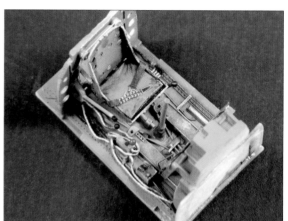

Eduard colour photoetch belts were used.

Wing detailing

As beautiful as this little kit is, it does not come with positionable flaps. I decided to correct this using some scratch building combined with the Verlinden update. The Verlinden set for the A6M2 is nice despite its relative age. The kit comes with photoetch and resin components that will allow you to drop flaps, and fold the wing tips as well as the rudder. I added bracing made from .010 Evergreen strip to the upper flap, but used the Verlinden brass framing for the lower flap. The folding wing tips from Verlinden are fine, but you will need to do your photo research before installing them. The brass pieces offered in Verlinden's kit are a bit clunky and inaccurate. I ended up using some Evergreen I-beam pieces to represent the hinge. The brass cutout for the wing fold does possess lightening holes; fine-gauge solder was used to represent hydraulic lines. In order to support the elliptical photoetch pieces in the wing cutouts, I used Evergreen plastic blocks on the backside of the part. When modifying the kit in this manner, be sure to include the fold-down brackets that deploy when the wing is folded.

A few key details were added to help make the aircraft more accurate. First, all Zeros involved in the Pearl Harbor attack carried aileron mass balances, painted red, on the bottom of the ailerons. On the wing upper surface, the kit has two recessed circles just inboard of the wing armament panels. The circle that is farthest inboard and forward is the wing fuel filler cap. The second circle, right next to the armament panel, is actually a small window used by the ground crew to check the armament bay. These were drilled out and filled with a small drop of Squadron Kristal Klear. After drying the Kristal Klear contracts, so I built this recess up with several applications of Future. Once dry, a bit more was dropped in with a fine point brush, until finally the windows were flush with the wing surface. Just inboard of the leading edge gun cover at the edge if the panel line I added some fine gauge steel wire to represent the landing gear status bar. This should be painted red with horizontal strips. The pitot on the kit was replaced with steel tubing, the larger part being a piece of Minimeca steel tubing, and the outer part coming from a syringe needle.

Ailerons, elevators and rudder

I used a Cutting Edge set for the elevators and the ailerons. They fitted nicely, though I did need to shim the rudder with some Evergreen after the cutting and cleaning process following removal from the resin block. All pieces were cut out by first scoring the panel line border of the control surface with a scribing tool and the backside of an X-acto knife with a No.11 blade.

Cowl flaps and Moskit exhaust stubs

I've always loved the precision appearance and finish of the exhaust stacks offered by Moskit. When I saw the exhausts for the Zero at the local hobby store, I knew I had to include them on the kit. In order to get them to fit, holes had to be drilled in the cowling where the kit pieces would normally be glued on. After playing with them a bit to get the correct angle, I applied a bead of glue on the inside of the cowling followed by a quick shot of Zip-kicker.

Since the kit cowl does not possess open cowl flaps, I decided to scratch-build the open flaps from Evergreen strip. I measured the size of the outer and inner cowl flap then cut them out of thin sheets of Evergreen. Gluing the individual flaps into position was tricky, as I wanted to make sure they all displayed the appropriate angles.

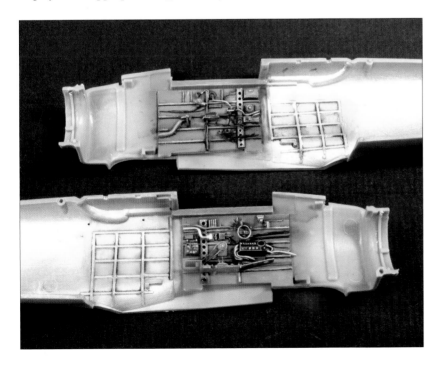

Cockpit sidewalls in place and painted.

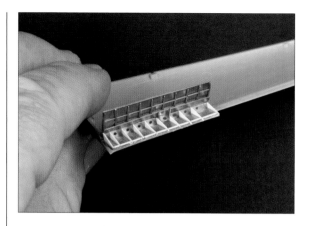

Ribs for the flaps were added to the Verlinden brass using plastic cut from Evergreen stock.

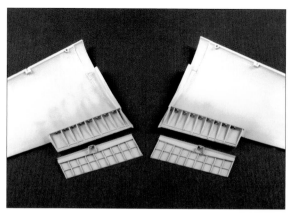

The flaps were painted in the cockpit colour. Subsequently, I discovered in discussion with Ryan Toews that the flaps would have been painted Exterior Green or *aotake*.

The wings were prepared for the folding of the wing tips by first cutting the wings along the panel lines. The plastic was then thinned using a burring tool in preparation for the addition of the photoetch façade.

Resin blocks were used to support the photoetch.

Folding wing details from the A6M3 being rebuilt in Chino.

Once the seams were filled, and the surface polished, the aircraft was pre-shaded with Burnt Umber.

Fuselage finishing and painting

Once the main sub-assemblies were finished, I began the paint preparation of the aircraft. I always check and double check to make sure all assembly seams are filled and sanded. If any panel lines are sanded off, they are put back using a scribing tool or an X-acto knife. In prepping for paint, I want to be certain that the surface is free of oils and is perfectly smooth. To achieve the latter, I wet-sand the surface starting with 400-grade paper and work my way down to 1,500 grit. I follow this with a thorough buffing of the surface with a Dremel tool mounting a laminated cotton polishing disc. I keep the drill on low, and manipulate the disc using the flexishaft Dremel tool extension.

I always start the painting by pre-shading panel lines (I use Burnt Umber with a drop of Black added to the cup). As mentioned before, this is done to give the final finish some depth. Pre-shading can easily ruin the look of your aircraft if it is not properly muted during the finishing process. My philosophy regarding pre-shading is that it should be noticed but not seen.

Once the pre-shading is complete, I paint the surface colours, starting with the lightest colour. When painting over the pre-shading, I do not attempt to cover the pre-shading. Rather, I paint the surface evenly, gradually covering it. I stop when the pre-shading is covered to the extent that it is no longer obviously visible but can be noticed as a gradual transition in tone. Next, I add a drop or two of a lighter colour to the paint cup. This can be done using Flat White, Yellow, Sand (also called Ivory by Testors) or Light Grey. Again, subtlety is the key. I make sure this 'new mix' is well thinned (about 70/30), and thin out the area within the various panels to give some contrast to the surface. As with the pre-shading, this is something that should be noticed but not seen. If the contrast is too great between the panels and panel lines, an unrealistic, 'quilted' finish is

The base coat of paint is put down lightly over the pre-shading. The colours used for top and bottom were Greg Springer's excellent mix of SAC Bomber Tan, Flat White and Zinc Chromate.

The trick in making use of the pre-shading is to add enough paint so the pre-shading is thoroughly covered, but not so much that it becomes irrelevant. The idea is for the pre-shading to be noticed but not seen.

After a protective coat of Future Floor Wax has been applied, the surface of the aircraft is given a liberal coat of artist oils Burnt Umber. If some gets outside the panel lines, the pigment can easily be rubbed away with a clean cloth. I use Q-tips.

The cowl flaps were cut out and replaced with thin strips of Evergreen card. The control surfaces were painted a lightened slate grey. The cowl was painted with White Ensign's Mitsubishi Cowl Blue-Black.

produced. If this happens, it can easily be corrected by spraying the over-lightened surface with a very thin mix of Clear Flat, tinted with a couple of drops of the surface colour. This will allow you to bring back your base colour a little at a time. Remember to keep these coats thin, otherwise you will end up with an orange-peel, or bumpy surface, characteristic of too many layers of paint.

There has been a great deal of recent research into Japanese naval aircraft colours. For this daunting task, I employed the assistance of Greg Springer, a regular and very helpful contributor to the J-aircraft.com web site, as well as Ryan Toews, who was personally involved in making sure the Blayd Zero was painted the correct colours. The infamous *Ameiro* or *Tsuchi-Iro* is a clear protective coating that was applied to the exterior (as well as wheel wells and the inside of gear doors of Mitsubishi-built Zeros) of many Japanese naval aircraft and almost all Zeros. Pearl Harbor Zeros were painted this colour on the upper and lower surfaces. In order to recreate this unique colour, the modeller has several options. A common choice for those who prefer acrylic paints is Floquil's 'old concrete'. I paint exclusively with enamels. Although White Ensign's line of Japanese aircraft colours includes this colour (Mitsubishi Zero Grey-Green ACJ16), I decided, after consulting with several people with 'normal' colour vision, to go with a mix of Testors Model Master colours graciously provided by Greg Springer. Mix Model Master's Flat White (part), SAC Bomber Tan (part) and Zinc Chromate (part). The accuracy of the mix is supported by the picture of the finished model sitting on a panel from the gear well of an A6M3 with the original paint still intact (see p.39).

Control surfaces were fabric and not painted in the *Ameiro* colour. Once again, Greg Springer came to the aid of this colour-blind modeller and suggested I use Testors Dark Slate Grey mixed with Flat White in a ratio of 2:1. I then highlighted this colour with Testors Pale Green.

Decals

Many of my friends mask and paint their own markings. Although this gives a fantastic final result, it is time consuming. I prefer to use good, thin decals and a lot of decal solvent. On this project I used the kit markings for a bird from the carrier *Akagi*. The *hinomaru* were taken from an Aeromaster *Hinomaru* sheet. My system for decaling always starts with a thorough coating of Future Floor Wax. This gives the finish a protective, smooth acrylic coat. Once the decals were properly positioned, they were flattened with a moistened sponge, and coated liberally with MicroSol. I usually end up applying several coats before I am satisfied. Once the decals were adequately pulled down over the surface, I applied another coat of Future over the decals. This helps to feather the decals into the surface.

The kit decals were used. They were in register and thin and went on with little fuss. A bit of MicroSol decal softener pulled them down very nicely into the panel lines. It is important to note that at this stage of the war these Zeros were well cared for. Massive amounts of weathering would be inappropriate. The aircraft would have had a glossy sheen, but this would be somewhat muted in a 1/48-scale model. I adjusted for scale by essentially spraying a semi-gloss on the model. The mix I used consisted of a 50/50 mix of Testors Clear Flat and Clear Gloss (thinned to a 50/50 ratio). The turtle decking behind the pilot should, of course, be Cowl Blue-Black and not Cockpit Green. I had to go back and fix this oversight later.

Weathering

It is important to note that although Japanese aircraft are famous for the extensive weathering they underwent (actually no greater than US aircraft in the same theatre), Pearl Harbor aircraft were in pristine condition during the raid. There would have been little or no gun burns (depending on whether you are modelling the aircraft before or after the raid); paint chipping would be nonexistent or extremely minimal (probably on wing walk areas if at all). The final finish on these Zeros should not be flat; these aircraft would be glossy overall. Be careful to take into consideration scaling; remember, the smaller the surface area, the less light will be reflected. I accomplished this subtle glossing by over-spraying the aircraft after the weathering process with a coat of Testors Clear Gloss (not as glossy as Future) with a couple of drops of Flat mixed in.

The weathering process always begins with a wash of artist's oils. There are two schools of thought regarding this process. One technique involves using a pin wash on a shiny surface. Once the wash begins to dry, it can easily be wiped off the surface using a clean cloth or a Q-tip. This keeps your surface paint clean with just a hint of contrasting colour in your panel lines. The second approach is the one I prefer, coating the entire model with Testors Clear Flat before the wash. Instead of a thin pin wash in the panel lines, I paint a thick layer of pigment into the lines. By thick I mean the consistency of the wash is still liquid, but dark and more viscous than you would use on a pin wash. When this dries, I use Q-tips dipped in Turpenoid to remove the pigment. Be sure to squeeze out the excess solvent with a cloth. This requires patience, and some nerve. The first time rubbing out the pigment, there may still be some pigment left in the lines and on the surface. Grab another Q-tip and wipe it out again! Keep going until there is little or no pigment transferred to the Q-tip when you wipe out the line. The reason I use Burnt Umber or Raw Umber rather than black is because black is a bit too contrasting. Once again, I am going for an impression of colour rather than a stark line. You will notice two things when you are done. You will see patches of gloss showing through your flat finish and possibly some residue solvent adjacent to your panels (leftover Turpenoid). Don't panic! Mix up a cup of Clear Flat (again, make sure it is thin) and spray your entire surface again. It is important to point out that Clear Flat can sometimes leave a 'fog' of white on the surface of your model. It looks almost

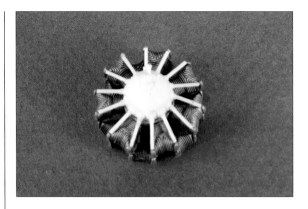

I found the CMK engine to be outstanding. In addition to the engine, the set includes top and bottom cowling pieces. I had hoped to display the model with the bottom cowling half sitting next to the model, and the top piece resting on top of the engine. Unfortunately I found after construction of the engine that the cowling didn't really fit properly on top of the engine. If you plan to use the CMK set, you will most likely need to set the cowling to the side of the engine. Ultimately, I decided to use the kit cylinders and the CMK crankcase.

A comparison of the kit and the CMK engine side by side. It is easy to see in this picture the diameter difference of the two engines.

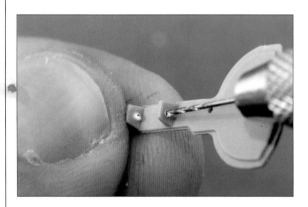

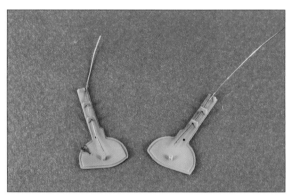

The kit gear doors were drilled out to accept some fine-gauge solder used to represent brake lines.

The solder brake lines.

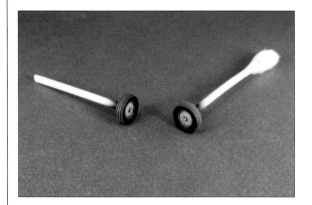

True Details wheels were used instead of the kit wheels.

CMK's gun sight was used. The aiming glass was added using some spare clear plastic sheet (I used the plastic containers new paint brushes come in).

like the yeast bloom you see on fruit at the grocery store. This is usually caused by the ratio of flattening agent/ clear in your bottle of Flat. If you get this fogging effect, simply grab your bottle of Testors Clear Gloss, and add a couple of drops to your cup, re-thin, and re-spray (but always test-spray first).

The undersurfaces of all operational aircraft were grubby, especially radial engine fighters. When weathering the bottom of the Zero, I chose to include a moderate amount of weathering that may have been present after the raid. To accomplish this, I placed a tiny dot of artist oil pigment in panel and then drew it back with a stroke of a flat-tipped weathering brush that was moist (not wet) with solvent. Too much solvent and you wipe the paint out. Not enough, and your streak looks like a glob. Another fantastic resource for this kind of weathering is MIG's dry pigments.

The kit guns and pitot were replaced with Minimeca tubing and cut syringe tubing.

The prop was painted with Model Master Buffable Aluminum, buffed out, and sprayed with a light protective coat of Future Floor Wax.

The antennae wire was made using clear nylon thread. I prefer using thread to using stretched sprue because of the durability of the thread. If you bump the wire, you are not likely to damage the thread. If you decided to use this material, be sure you have some cyanoacrylate accelerator (I use Zipkicker), as superglue alone will not hold this wire tight.

Subtle post-shading of the wing panels really brings the model to life. As always, it is prudent to underdo rather than overdo the effect, especially on aircraft that were so well cared for.

The fuselage of the finished model.

ABOVE The folded wing tips really add life to the model.

BELOW In this photo, the model is sitting on a gear well panel from an A6M3 Zero being restored by Vintage Aircraft Ltd. in Ft Collins, Colorado. The original paint, which would be the same for the exterior, is a close match to the Greg Springer mix I used for the model.

Captured A6M5b, TAIC No.7 (1/32)

Subject:	*A6M5b in the markings of TAIC No.7; a captured Zero*
Modeller:	*Brian Criner*
Skill level:	*Master*
Base kit:	*Tamiya A6M5b*
Scale:	*1/32*
Additional detailing sets used:	*CMK wheels/wing fuel tanks/tail wheel accessories/open panels and panel covers on wings and fuselage sides/engine crankcase and backing/gun bays, Eduard coloured belts, and various cockpit details.*
Additional detailing materials used:	*Evergreen plastic rod; fine-gauge solder; fine-gauge copper wire; Minimeca tubing; Evergreen plastic card; fine-gauge steel wire.*
Decals:	*Cutting Edge; CAM; and others.*
Paints:	*Tamiya acrylics: Clear Blue; Clear Red.* *Model Master Enamels: SAC Bomber Tan; Flat White; Zinc Chromate; Flat Black.* *Model Master Buffable Metalizer: Aluminum; Stainless Steel; Titanium; Dark Anodenic Gray.*

When I first considered writing this book, I knew the Tamiya 1/32-scale A6M5 Zero would have to be the centrepiece. I had built the kit before, so I knew how well engineered it was and how nicely it went together. My only concern was what scheme to do? Essentially my choices were green over grey – or green over grey! As I was sharing this idea with my friend Stan one day, he jumped out of his chair and exclaimed, 'I know what scheme you are going to do!' He started describing an article that he had seen in *Fine Scale Modeller* years ago (Vol. 12, No. 2, February 1994). The article, written by Daniel Garsonnin, describes a technique for recreating the stressed-skin look of real aircraft on a scale model. I immediately said 'no'. As I remembered it, the technique involved 'carving up' the skin of the kit, rescribing lines, and adding back rivets by hand or through the use of a tool called a pounce wheel. That all sounded far too difficult. 'Yeah, but think of how cool it will look,' said Stan, acting as devil's advocate. Later, I found several articles on Hyperscale.com by a modeller named Jaroslav Galler detailing his methods for recreating this kind of a finish. Jaroslav was kind enough to send me several photos demonstrating his technique as well as an explanation of how he was able to achieve his amazing finishes. Long story short: I decided in fear and trembling to go forward with the project. Fred Medel from Tamiya USA graciously donated a kit and some extra fuselages and wing sprues, which meant I had more than enough backup for when things went wrong.

In order to really show off this finish, I decided to model a Zero, TAIC No.7, captured on the island of Saipan. This is the same aircraft that is hanging in the National Air and Space Museum. This aircraft carried several schemes over the course of its career as an American aircraft, some of them quite striking. However, I decided to go for one that would show off the natural metal finish in the best way possible.

Cockpit

The Tamiya cockpit is a beautiful piece of engineering. Like most Tamiya kits, the fit is fabulous. There are a few shortcomings though. The cockpit appears to be patterned after a captured Zero, as the radio is incorrect for an A6M5 (see Ryan Toew's article on the Tamiya Zero on J-aircraft.com), though it is correct for the Zero I was doing. I began by modifying the cockpit. I added various sizes of speaker wire and fine-gauge solder to represent the extensive wiring found on the sidewalls and floor of the cockpit.

Cockpit walls

Wiring was added to the electrical control panel using fine-gauge beading wire (used for making necklaces and bracelets) found at a craft store. The nice thing about beading wire, other than the variety of sizes it comes in, is its ability to maintain a curve when bending. This is helpful when constructing the electrical panel as the wires loop out and down below the panel. I drilled out holes in the sidewall framing and looped copper wire through to hold the curve in the wire. The throttle quadrant linkage bars were added using stiff steel wire. The throttle handle should be painted light blue (I initially painted mine brown). A very thin, very nice throttle is provided in the Eduard set. It is a bit tricky to assemble and I ended up bending mine beyond recognition, so I went with the kit quadrant. A photoetch chain from Eduard was added to the trim control wheel. The flat propeller pitch control handle is also from Eduard. Wiring was added to the right wall using beading wire and I fastened the framing using copper wire.

Fuselage floor

The Tamiya floor is nicely done, but can still benefit from a few fixes. First, the small control box in the front right portion of the floor was drilled out to represent the lightening holes. A small, star-shaped photoetched gear was placed in the front centre of the rudder bar. Linkage bars which were connected to the rudder pedals were added using pieces of steel wire. I cut small pieces of solder and glued them to the ends of some copper wire that was inserted into the top of the box to represent the various handles. The hydraulic gear and wiring on the lower right side of the cockpit was represented using copper wire and solder. Photoetch foot straps from Eduard were added to the rudder pedals. Control boxes on the lower left of the cockpit were also improved with copper wire.

Instrument panel

I used the kit-provided film for the instrument panel. I started by painting the panel in cockpit colours and then picking out details with a fine point brush. After a coat of Future and coat of Flat, a wash of Burnt Umber was applied. Fine bits of scuffing were represented by drawing them in with a fine point Chrome Berol Prismacolor pencil. After the panel was finished and the instrument film was added to the back, I placed a small drop of Future Floor Wax in each dial. After a while, when the 'bubble' of Future had dried and contracted, I added another. The process was repeated until a convex bubble of clear was present in each dial face. Some wires were added to the bottom of the panel to finish it off.

Rear bulkhead and seat

CMK makes a beautifully detailed seat with harnesses moulded into it. I elected to go with the kit seat and coloured photoetch belts provided by Eduard. I had always been fairly certain the Zero seats had only lap harnesses. Ryan Toews pointed out that this Zero would have probably possessed a shoulder harness as well. The oxygen tanks in the back of the bulkhead were the kit parts with lightening holes drilled to make them appear more authentic. Copper wire was

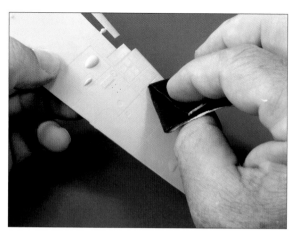

The scalloping process begins by scraping out all of the panel lines and rivets with a small, elliptically edged blade. I am using a micro-dissection scalpel obtained from a science lab supply company. They are inexpensive and come in packages of 5 to 10 blades each. You can also use No.15 disposable scalpel blades. The 'line' cut by the blade need not be perfectly straight.

Once the panel lines were scraped out, wet-dry sandpaper was used to smooth out the edges of the grooves. Missing rivet holes were replaced using a sewing needle in a pin vice. My friend Rian Jones actually sent me a very nice pounce wheel for this project, but I felt I would have better control using the pin vice.

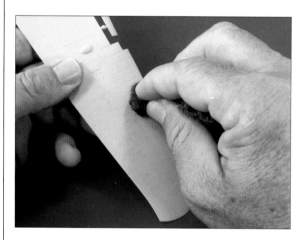

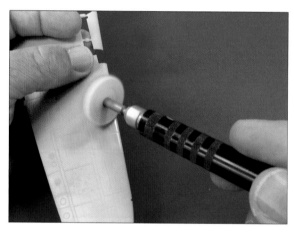

Once fine scratches were removed, the model was further cleaned up using fine steel wool and polishing cloth.

ABOVE, BELOW LEFT AND RIGHT AND OPPOSITE TOP LEFT
Once the part is polished out with the buffing wheel, the finish has a glass-like sheen.

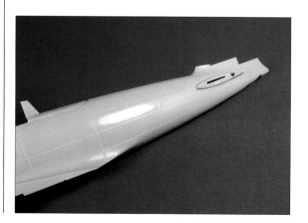

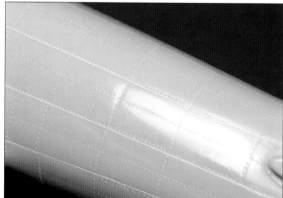

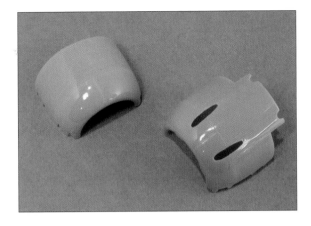

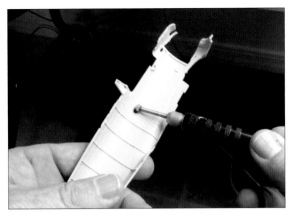

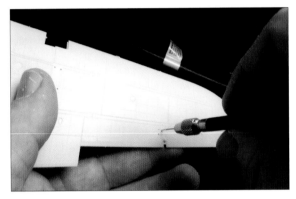

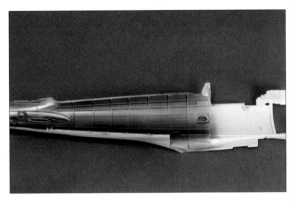

ABOVE AND TOP RIGHT Following the polishing process, all panels that were to be detailed were cut out and the backsides thinned in preparation for the addition of the resin inserts.

Before closing the fuselage and wings up, all inner faces were sprayed *aotake*. This unique finish was replicated by first spraying Aluminum, followed by a coat of Tamiya Clear Blue. The final coat is Tamiya Clear Green. Adjust the amount of green you add by considering the amount of exposure the part had to the environment.

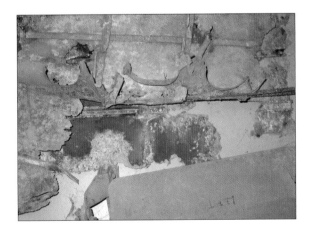

From inspections of original paint on an A6M3 being refurbished by Vintage Aircraft Ltd. in Ft Collins, Colorado, it appears that greater exposure to air caused the *aotake* preservative to change to an almost 'candy apple' green.

The 'actual' *aotake* colour is nicely represented by a piece of cockpit sheet metal taken from the A6M3 being refurbished in Ft Collins. It is interesting to note that this was an area that was protected from exposure to air because it was sandwiched between two pieces of metal. Compare the colour to the piece that has experienced prolonged exposure on the left.

added to the tanks and some more Eduard pieces were employed to represent the various parts of the bulkhead. Lightening holes in the seat retraction mechanism and in the seat supports were recreated with a drill and pin vice. The bungee cord attached to the back of the seat was represented by drilling holes in the base of the seat and threading fine-gauge beading wire into the hole. The beading wire was bonded with a drop of Zap and then threaded around the two, round bulkhead rollers at the top of the bulkhead and glued into the opposite side of the seat.

Forward firewall, engine mount and oil tank

I discovered (too late) that the oil tank mounted in front of the firewall should be painted natural metal finish silver. I thought I had heard of one being painted in black or blue-black, so that is how I finished it. There are several wires that lead out of the firewall and I'm not sure where they go – but I wasn't too concerned about it, as I knew this area would be difficult to see in the completed model. The large tubing extending out of the top and bottom of the oil tank was made from solder, the smaller wires from copper speaker wire. Moskit provides a wonderful little update that includes the air vent in the starboard leading edge wing and the blast tubes for the cowling guns. The blast tubes were a little over-size for the bulkhead opening, so I opened this up with a drill bit in a pin vice. All of the wiring in the cockpit and bulkhead looks great, but with Tamiya's meticulous engineering there isn't a lot of extra room under the cockpit floor; a lot of test-fitting is necessary before mating the fuselage halves and the wing bottom all together.

Wings and control surfaces

I decided to open up flap and aileron actuator panels, gun bays, and the lower fuel cell bays. I used the CMK update set, which comes with resin boxes containing nicely moulded actuator rods as well as photoetch fasteners. Because these pieces need to be glued to the inner wing halves, considerable grinding, using the Dremel tool with a grinding bit inserted, was involved. Once the resin pieces were painted and the photoetch was in place, the pieces were glued to the inner surface. There is a lot of resin in the wing, which meant much test-fitting. In order to get the fuel cells to fit, I had to carve away a significant amount of the moulded-in inner wing space.

The gun bays were a little trickier. I was able to fit them easily into the opening I cut into the wing, but experienced some problems getting them to fit with the kit gear wells. I decided to go with the kit pieces over the CMK pieces because I felt the fit of the CMK wells was not as good as that of the kit parts. Once I was able to get a good fit with the kit parts, I found after test-fitting that the resin pieces sat too high in the wing. This meant that the gun barrel would not fit through the hole in the wing once the bay was installed. With more test-fitting as well as some shimming of the gun bays with plasticard, I was able to get all of the pieces in place and the wing glued together with few problems.

In order to get the Moskit ventilation tube to fit in the starboard wing leading edge, I needed to carve out the opening in the wing edge first. This was easy enough, as there were some moulded-in panel lines to mark its location. It was also necessary to grind a trough in the backside of the kit gear well to create a seat for the tube. While working on the trough, I also drilled out the lightening holes that are so prominent in Zero wheel bays. I originally tried assembling the Eduard wheel bays, for which you need to cut out all of the cross-bracing at the bottom of the gear bay. The parts looked great, but did not fit well in the wing, making it difficult to close the wing halves together. Since I had already made up the kit pieces I used them instead. Detailing the wheel wells involved creating a gear retraction mechanism with springs attached. In

The Tamiya cockpit is nicely detailed, needing nothing in the way of aftermarket upgrades. There are minor errors that the modeller may want to address; these corrections are nicely outlined and addressed in an article by Ryan Toews that can be found on www.J-aircraft.com. The cockpit wiring was reproduced using fine-gauge beading wire obtained from a craft store. What makes beading wire an attractive choice for this application is that it is a very fine metallic weave sheathed in clear plastic. The plastic prevents the wire from kinking, so it is excellent for replicating curved wires. All cockpit wiring in the Zero should be painted silver. I chose to paint some of the wiring black to give the floor some contrast.

BELOW AND BOTTOM
The finished cockpit pieces before installation. After installation of the cockpit I was informed by Ryan Toews that this aircraft would probably have had a single shoulder belt.

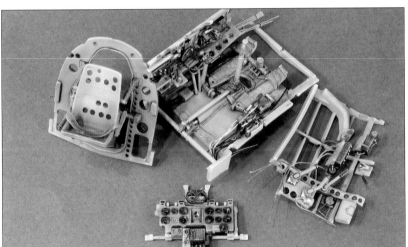

order to affix the springs, first I needed two strong pieces to attach the two ends. I found a couple of pieces on a spare photoetch sheet that looked right. After fixing their shape a bit with an X-acto knife, I glued them in place. This was followed by an agonizing hour in which I had to thread the ends of the mini-springs through the holes in the photoetch pieces. Since I seem to be committed to doing things in the most difficult manner possible, I actually attempted this after I had the plane assembled!

Preparing the fuselage

In preparation for adding those great CMK pieces, it was necessary to modify the fuselage. I began by thinning the inside of the fuselage behind the gun charging system panel on the left fuselage half. Care must be taken here so that the moulded-in ribbing is not destroyed. I thinned the fuselage using a small grinding bit on the Dremel tool. A lot of test-fitting was necessary here to ensure the resin piece was seated properly. Holes were drilled on this side to accommodate the styrene rod used to represent boarding steps. One step I forgot and had to complete later was the addition of a hole to the left of the panel.

The open tail fairing is a nice addition by CMK. I carefully cut this part off the kit using the Dremel, scribing tools and an X-acto knife. After clean up, I inserted the resin bulkhead provided in the CMK set. It is important to point out here that on the real aircraft there is no bulkhead. It is open, and the hydraulic retraction cylinder simply extends into the opening. The problem you encounter by leaving this area open is that it makes the interior of the fuselage visible, specifically the moulded-in, round grommet holder that is used for the moveable tailplanes. Unfortunately, this didn't occur to me until after the fuselage pieces were mated together. If you would like to create a more accurate open tail, you could forgo the moveable tailplane, grind out the grommet holders, and add ribbing using styrene.

Creating the scalloping effect

This is a nerve-wracking process. Taking a scalpel and carving up a perfectly good (and expensive) kit smacks of insanity. However, with my notes from Jaroslav and my copy of the *Fine Scale Modeller* article (not to mention my extra wings and fuselage pieces) I jumped in. I began with the left fuselage half. I simply took my scalpel and began carving out the panel lines and rivets. I made use of a micro-dissection scalpel with a small, sharp, stainless steel blade for this task; the blade has a very small, fine curve. I tried to keep my strokes with the blade even. I wanted the cut to have a shallow depth, and the lip of the cut should have a gradual taper. Initially you will be horrified by how terrible it looks. Be patient and persevere – it will get better!

After carving out my panel lines (on the Tamiya kit they are more like lines of dots than actual lines), I put a sewing needle into a pin vice and put all of those rivet holes back by hand – prepare yourself, this will take a while. As an alternative, you could use a tool called a pounce wheel to put the rivets back in. Once the rivet holes were back in, I began to wet sand the surfaces. Starting with 400-grit sandpaper, I gradually worked my way up to a 12,000-grit polishing cloth. By this time, the surface of the model was quite shiny.

At this point I carefully looked over the entire surface of the pieces that I was modifying to check for mistakes. Any lines that were C-shaped needed their edges sanding down. Rough spots were smoothed out. This is the part of the build that requires a real investment of time and patience. You simply have to tell yourself you will not go forward until the surface looks the way it ought to. Note that in order to get the proper finish here, it is important to use liquid gap filler like Zap, rather than the grainy types carried by Squadron and Tamiya; these may look right before you paint, but painting an NMF surface is different – spraying Metalizer over grainy putty just doesn't work.

The Tamiya instrument panel is beautifully done. The gauges are photo-film on the back of a clear plastic insert. Each dial face received several drops of Future Floor Wax in order to maintain a nice glossy appearance. Simulated wiring was added to the base of the panel using beading wire.

Firewall detail from the 'Russian' A6M3 at Chino.

The Tamiya firewall was jazzed up with the addition of fine-gauge solder obtained from the local hardware store. The firewall was plumbed with medium-gauge solder and copper wiring taken from speaker wires. The cowl gun blast tubes are Moskit products. In order to get them to fit it is necessary to open up the holes in the firewall just a bit. Some of the rear cockpit detail can be seen in this photo. As this area is nearly invisible in the finished kit, less time was spent detailing the area.

Despite being a royal pain, the scalloping and polishing process produces dramatic and worthwhile results.

Take your time with this stage of the process. It will be taxing, but the results speak for themselves.

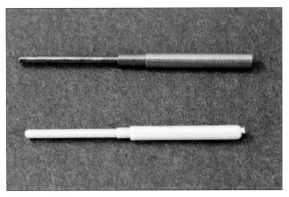

The kit pitot, though decent, was improved using Minimeca tubing and fine-gauge syringe needles.

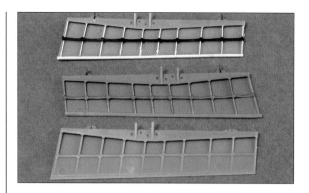

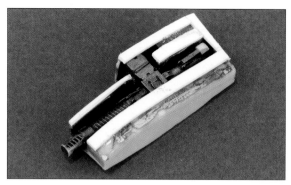

In this photo you can see the stock kit flap on the bottom and the modified flaps above. After the modified flap was built, it was sprayed with Mr. Surfacer 1000 as shown with the flap in the middle.

The CMK gun bays did not fit properly in the wing. The kit instructions suggest you should glue the bays to the inside surface of the upper wing. Unfortunately, after the upper wing had been thinned to achieve scale thickness, the gun bay sat too high. If you close the wings and try to insert the barrel, the gun will be too high for the barrel. After a bit of test-fitting and shimming the parts with some Evergreen sheet I was able to get the bay to fit.

CMK fuel bays installed in wing. Wing spares were painted with Testors Metalizer Stainless Steel.

Once the fuselage and wing were mated, and all seams and joints were properly blending or filled, the cockpit was masked off and the entire model was coated with Mr. Surfacer 1000. Once the Mr. Surfacer was dry, the model was buffed out again with the polishing wheel until a nice sheen was obtained.

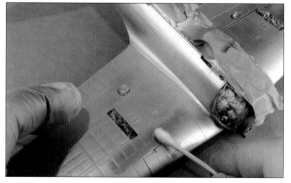

Painting a natural metal finish using Model Master Buffable paint is tricky, but the process will give you a unique and convincing finish. After masking all relevant areas with Tamiya tape, the model was sprayed with a coat of Aluminum.

The model was then lightly buffed with a Q-tip and then thoroughly buffed with the Dremel tool on the lowest speed. Though it seems this will damage the paint, it actually creates a beautiful metallic sheen.

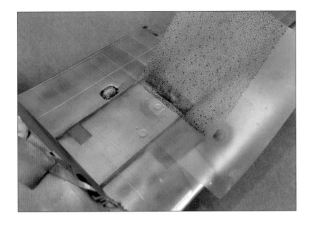

Various panels and hatches were masked off using low-tack watercolour artist's tape and frisket film obtained from an art supply store. Pulling up even low-tack tape should be done with care using this system, as the paint is very fragile.

There was some damage to the underlying paint due to masking, but it was easily repaired and carefully re-sprayed.

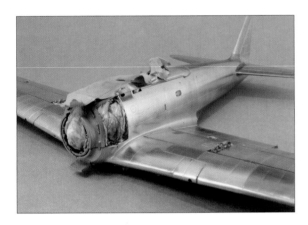

The model is buffed out again with the polishing wheel. If there is a primer coat of Mr. Surfacer on the model, and the model is carefully buffed, you are not likely to damage the paint. If, by chance, the surface is damaged in this process, a repair coat can easily be applied (provided you haven't decaled yet).

Decals were obtained from the spares box.

The tail markings were measured and cut from spare 1/24-scale Trumpeter *hinomaru*.

Moskit part 32-08 provides beautifully realistic exhaust stacks. If you track down any of these hard-to-find gems at the local hobby store, buy them up! They are expensive, but worth it.

The kit engine is nice. Despite the availability of a very nice update set from CMK, I decided to use the kit cylinders combined with the CMK engine back. The wiring harness was detailed by first drilling out the kit piece with a fine drill bit and then adding various sizes of solder. Cylinder head braces were recreated using sections of Evergreen rod cut to the appropriate size.

The finished engine, right side view. Even though the rear of the engine is practically invisible once installed, I decided to jazz it up using several different gauges of solder.

The finished engine, rear view.

The finished engine, left side view.

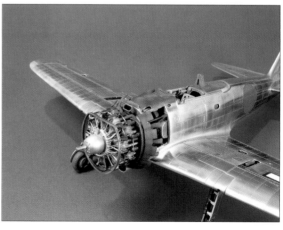

The finished engine, rear view.

The locating tabs on the back of the engine fit into holes on the engine mount.

Once the model had had all of its rivet and panels replaced and seams filled, I buffed the entire surface with a laminated, stitched polishing disc in the Dremel, taking care not to burn the plastic. Once the model was buffed to a mirror-like sheen, I sprayed Mr. Surfacer 1000 over the entire surface. This part of the process is necessary as the Metalizer will quickly wear off if not properly primed. After the Mr. Surfacer had dried, I buffed the model to a glossy sheen. The polishing wheel can even remove rough angles in the scalloping if done right. Unfortunately, burning the plastic occasionally happens, but don't worry: the skin on Zeros was thin and became quite warped, bent and twisted after several flying hours were put on the aircraft. Simply sand off the rough edges of your 'burnt' area, and then polish again, starting with very fine grade wet-dry paper (800 grit), and finishing with the very fine polishing cloth. When I was sure that the surface was ready, I began painting.

Painting with Metalizer

I had a number of choices for creating a natural metal finish, but decided to go with Testors Metalizer. I chose it because once buffed out, it gives the most realistic metallic lustre. True, these aircraft were not 'showroom new' when they were tested, but the lustre was present, at least on parts of the aircraft. Using Metalizer is frustrating and tedious at times (you must always wear gloves when handling the model), but the durability of the paint is greatly enhanced by the use of Mr. Surfacer as a primer.

Once the entire model had been covered in Buffable Aluminum, I lightly rubbed it out with a Q-tip. Next, the model was buffed with the polishing disc and Dremel tool. This rubs the paint into the surface and gives the model a beautiful metallic lustre. In order to create the multi-hue finish characteristic of natural metal aircraft, I began to mask off various areas of the aircraft. When masking Metalizer, it is important to use a very low-tack tape. I took a trip down to the local Hobby Lobby art store in my area, and found some low-tack tape used by watercolour artists. I used this tape to mask off long lines, such as the wing space, and Post-It notes to mask small, square panels on the wing. I made sure to pull the tape up slowly. I did get some paint pulled off by the tape, but it was the surface layer only. This is where I discovered the benefits of using Mr. Surfacer. In the past, when Metalizer was pulled up by tape, it took all of the paint up, right down to the surface. When painting this Zero, there was not a single instance in which that occurred. I did end up with a few fingerprints here and there as well as some discolouration from the tape, but I simply buffed it out again with the Dremel. It goes without saying that great care must be taken with this step. Any 'burns' inflicted by the polishing wheel will be much more difficult to fix at this point.

Decaling

I had originally decided to mask and paint my markings. With my decision to use Metalizer, though, I realized this was not a good idea considering the fragility of the finish. I had used the Tamiya decals provided in the kit in the past, and I found them too thick. I decided to go with *hinomaru* from a Cutting Edge sheet as well as a CAM decal sheet that Armand, the owner of CAM, had given me at a recent contest. The decals went on nicely, and needed only a small amount of MicroSol to get them to sit. Be careful not to allow the MicroSol to drip in large amounts onto your painted surface. Although it does not dissolve paint, it does have the tendency to stain it, which is difficult to clean later on. For the aircraft code numbers on the empennage, I used numbers from a decal sheet with only numbers and letters. For the TAIC markings on the tail, I pieced the letters together from the label on a Promodeller decal sheet for the Ta 154. The bright red 'swoosh' on the tail was cut from the large *hinomaru* provided in the Trumpeter Zero kit. The 'Tokyo Rose' letters were taken from a sheet of aircraft letters and numbers. This particular aircraft apparently carried several different markings. The

With all of the extra wiring in the back of the engine, getting it to fit properly was a challenge.

The prop was painted natural metal with no bands, though the actual aircraft most likely possessed warning bands on the tips of the propeller blades. I stuck with the plain metal blade because I thought it looked good. I pray the god of modelling accuracy doesn't strike me down for my sin!

The added detail really makes a difference to the final appearance of the engine.

However, the engine back detail is hardly visible in the finished product.

A real dilemma was how to weather the aircraft without damaging the fragile finish. Normally, I cover the finish with a protective coat of Future Floor Wax, and then apply a thin wash of oil-based pigments. Spraying a protective coat of Future would have worked, but it would have dulled the finish and ruined the effect of the Metalizer. I decided, after some encouragement from a friend, to use MIG pigments on my finish.

At first glance, MIG pigment looks like pastel dust. That is where the similarities end. This beautiful product is composed of ground-up pigments that are soft and pliable and can easily be worked into the surface detail without scratching the paint.

mix of American Stars and Bars plus *hinomaru* is documented in at least one photo of this aircraft that I obtained from Jim Long. TAIC No.7 actually had natural metal cowl flaps and cowl fasteners. In the photo of a different captured bird, TAIC No.8, flown and tested at Ontario Army air base (today it is Ontario International Airport), the cowl flaps and fasteners were black, like the anti-glare panel. Though this configuration may not be perfectly accurate, I liked the overall appearance and decided to use artistic licence.

Weathering

Weathering a natural metal surface is like tap dancing on a frozen pond on a sunny day. Having spent so much time achieving a beautiful finish, choosing the wrong weathering technique would be a disaster to say the least. Typically, I coat the surface with Future Floor Wax to protect the paint, followed by a wash with artist oils. Covering Metalizer with any kind of protective clear coat destroys the very effect that makes it such a great choice. Future Floor Wax, Testors Clear Flat and even the protective coat made by Testors specifically for Metalize (Testors Metalizer Sealer) dulls the finish. So, washes are out.

While visiting Mission Models in Los Angeles, one of the guys behind the counter described a product used by armour modellers for weathering called MIG Pigments. I decided to buy a variety of different colours and see if I could use them for the Zero. Somewhat sceptically, I assumed this stuff would give the dry, dusty, easily damaged finish characteristic of pastels. MIG pigments actually go on smooth, with a slightly oily texture (without the residue). Essentially they are dried, ground-up oil pigments. When I applied them to the surface of the Metalizer, they easily stuck to the inside of panels and rivet depressions. When it was time to remove the excess, no solvent was required. I simply wiped it out with a dry Q-tip. I even buffed the surface with the polishing wheel and Dremel without damaging the finish. The surface was returned to its shine, and the buffing did not remove the pigment from the recesses.

In preparation for painting exhaust and oil staining, I mixed up a cup of Clear Flat with a few drops of Raw Sienna, Flat Black and Testors Sand added to the cup. The key to spraying on your weathering without it looking overdone is to keep the mix well thinned and to use a minimum of pigment. Test-spraying is essential here. The spray must come out feathered with no speckling (if you can see individual dots of paint, it needs more thinning). Whenever I spray this mix on the model, I am careful to make sure there is bright backlighting on the model. This allows me to keep track of exactly

Once the pigment had been worked into the recessed detail, the excess was merely wiped off with a Q-tip.

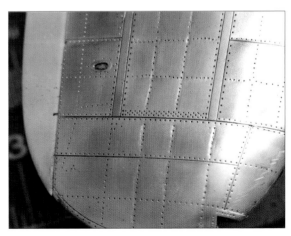

The finished result.

where, and how much, paint is making contact with the model. I carefully sprayed the exhaust pattern backwards from the exhaust stacks, being careful to consider how the slipstream of air moving over the wing would affect the pattern. I concentrated more pigment directly behind the stack, then slowly moved the airbrush away from the model surface the farther back I went. I used the same technique to simulate staining behind the wing guns, and the area on the bottom of the aircraft, directly behind the engine. Every picture I've seen of operational Zeros shows them heavily stained along the bottom (this Zero was of course, not operational, but it was flown like it was – most photos show it heavily stained). An added benefit to spraying this area with Flat is it changes how the MIG pigments appear on the surface of the model. Instead of being easily wiped out, more of the pigment stays behind on the flat surface. This gives the aircraft a unique and varied finish.

Additional weathering was applied with an airbrush and a Berol chrome coloured pencil. Exhaust stains were sprayed using a very thin mix of Testors Clear Flat, and approximately two drops of brown, one drop of tan and one drop of black. The thin ratio was about 55–60 per cent thinner to pigment. I always test-spray on a piece of white paper or card stock before it goes on the model. Any splattering of paint means the mix is too thick. I believe it is particularly important to keep this part of the weathering process subtle. I spray the exhaust staining in almost imperceptible layers, slowly building up the effect. The Berol pencil was used to add 'scuff' marks into the stains. Berol pencils have a waxy tip; they are difficult to use on glossy surfaces, but flat surfaces are easier.

Though CMK provides very nicely done wheel wells, I elected to use the kit wells. Lightening holes were carefully drilled out and a trough was created in the starboard well to allow for installation of the Moskit cockpit ventilation ducting.

LEFT In addition, gear door retraction springs were added using examples I stole from my friend Stan Spooner (I wonder if he's noticed them missing yet).

RIGHT You can see here a nice representation of an actual wheel well on an A6M3 being refurbished in Chino, California.

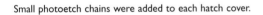
Small photoetch chains were added to each hatch cover.

Boarding steps and grab handles were made from thin sections of Evergreen rod.

The wing leading edge gun covers didn't fit properly, so some minor grinding was necessary along the inside edge of the covers in order for them to fit flush against the wing.

CMK offers a resin bulkhead onto which the tail wheel retraction strut is glued. On the real Zero there is no bulkhead structure. The retraction strut passes into the rear of the fuselage, which is open. Recreating this on the model would have been problematic, but not impossible. It would require removing the recesses on the inside of the fuselage where the rubber 'holdfast' grommets hold the moveable elevators. I elected to use the bulkhead because it just seemed like a more practical way to mount the tail wheel.

One complication that resulted from attempting this sort of finish is figuring out a method for applying markings that won't damage it. I had originally considered using stencils cut from frisket to mask off the markings. This proved to be a frustrating approach because the frisket either had too much tack, causing damage to the finish when removing the mask, or not enough tack, in which case spraying the markings would leave considerable overspray. After a few frustrating repair sessions (and a lot of cursing) I elected to go with decals for markings. The trick here is to cut the decals as close as possible to the markings.

The finished cockpit area.

Panel covers are resin offerings from the CMK set. The chains attaching the covers are photoetch pieces.

ABOVE **A frontal port side view of the finished model.**   BELOW **A frontal starboard side view of the Zero.**

ABOVE **A rear starboard view.**

BELOW **The front of the Zero with the cowl removed.**

Zero gallery

A6M3-22, Tainan Air Group (1/48)

Subject:	*Tainan Air Group A6M3 model 22 (flown by Hiroyoshi Nishizawa – the IJN's 'ace of aces')*
Modeller:	*Steve Kays*
Base kit:	*Hasegawa A6M3-22*
Scale:	*1/48*
Additional detailing sets used:	*Hawkeye resin interior, True Details resin wheels, CMK resin seat, EZ Mask canopy masks.* *Evergreen plastic rod* *Fine gauge solder* *Fine gauge copper wire*
Paints:	*Aeromaster: IJN orange-yellow. Tamiya acrylics: Mitsubishi Navy Green, Navy Grey/Green, Navy Interior Green, Clear Blue, Clear Red, Cowl Black. Model Master Enamels: SAC Bomber Tan, Flat White, Zinc Chromate. Alclad: Aluminum.*

Weathering was kept to a minimum on this model. Although weathering your model with chips, oil and smoke stains can be convincing, it can also be easily overdone. Wing leading edge ID bands were painted with an old bottle of Aeromaster enamel Japanese ID yellow-orange. The prop front and the spinner were painted with Alclad Aluminium. The top surface green mottle was field applied by crews during the war, and was painted in a variety of different patterns. The topside green was painted using Tamiya's Navy Green acrylic thinned approximately 70/30.

ABOVE The tyres were painted Flat Black and then post-shaded with successively lighter layers of grey. The powder burns on the wing from the gun were created using a thinned mix of Tamiya Smoke. It is essential when attempting to recreate this type of effect that you err on the side of caution. Over-weathering is a good way to ruin the finish on a perfectly good model. It is easier to add more later than to remove excess.

ABOVE RIGHT Fuselage *hinomaru* were created using an old wheel half as a guide to make a stencil. Once the stencil was created using Tamiya tape, the centre cutout section of the stencil was placed over the *hinomaru* and used as a mask when the topside green mottle was painted on.

In late 1941 an updated version of the Zero was undergoing flight trials. The A6M3-32 had a more powerful 1,130 hp Sakae 21 engine; a more symmetrical cowling was used that relocated the air intake from the bottom to the top of the cowl; and the folding wing tips were removed to counter the increase in weight that resulted from the new engine. Ultimately, the model 32's performance improvement over the model 21 was minimal, and range was actually reduced due to the reduction in wing fuel capacity and the increase in fuel consumption by the more powerful engine. In early 1942 it was decided to restore the extended wing tips and add 12-gallon fuel tanks to each wing of the A6M3. The A6M3 model 22, as this aircraft was designated, became one of the best performing Zeros. Performance and range were increased, and production began in autumn 1942.

One of the most famous pilots of the Japanese Naval Air Force was Warrant Officer Hiroyoshi Nishizawa. Together with Ensign Saburo Sakai and Petty Officer Toshio Otu, these three Tainan Air Group pilots became famous as the 'clean up trio' on the island of Lae, thanks to their incredible successes against Allied pilots. Probably one of the most famous wartime air-to-air photos of the

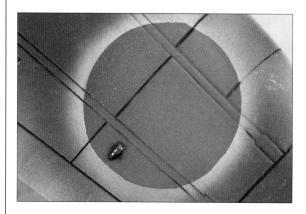

Formation lights were first painted with Testors Chrome Silver. Once the paint had dried thoroughly, the silver was painted over with a drop of the appropriate colour of Tamiya Clear.

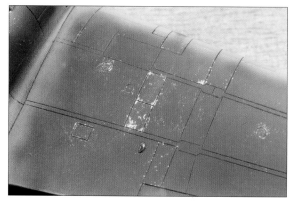

Final weathering was accomplished using a Berol silver pencil sharpened to a very fine point. Access panels and high-use areas were addressed using this technique. The nice thing about using the Berol pencils is the ease with which you can remove the effect if you don't like it.

Zero is a shot of Nishizawa flying an A6M3-22 sporting a dark green 'squiggle' pattern over the lighter *Tsuchi-Iro*. This 'defensive' camouflage was field applied, apparently without a set pattern.

Steve Kays used the Hasegawa A6M3 for this build, and only a few modifications were incorporated. The Hawkeye resin interior update was used for this build. The seat was updated with Eduard coloured belts. The model was pre-shaded, painted, and then post-shaded with a lightened version of the surface colour. The topside squiggle green was painted on using Tamiya Navy Green. The surface was then given an oil wash. Markings were a mix of decals and painted markings. Final weathering was done using a silver/metallic Berol Prismacolor pencil.

A6M5b Zero (1/32)

Subject:	*A6M5b Zero*
Modeller/photos:	*Brian Criner*
Base kit:	*Tamiya*
Scale:	*1/32*
Additional detailing sets used:	*Eduard photoetch*
Decals:	*Cutting Edge*

When Tamiya originally announced they were releasing a Zero in 1/32 scale several years ago, I decided I would dump whatever I was working on at the time and start straight away on it. The model was slightly modified for inclusion in this book. When it was originally built I was unaware of the fact that all Zeros were primed and had, right to the end of the war, very durable and wear-resistant paint jobs. So, I endeavoured to make a minor correction on my old build. I used a crimson red Berol coloured pencil and 'drew in' some residue priming on top of the paint chips. The only extras added to this model were some photoetch pieces from Eduard and decals from Cutting Edge.

The model was painted with Model Master Military Enamels. In order to create the 'chipping' effect, the model was first undercoated with Testors Buffable Aluminum, buffed to a shine with a Dremel polishing wheel and then given a protective coat of Future Floor Wax. The model was then pre-shaded, painted with the surface colours, and then post-shaded with lighted versions of the surface colours. Once the painting was finished, the model was 'chipped' by pressing rolled-up pieces of regular masking tape against the surface. Weathering was done by adding just one or two drops of the desired pigment (Black or Brown for staining, White or Tan for simulating paint fading) to a paint cup filled with Clear Flat. The mix is thoroughly thinned (about 70/30) and sprayed at a slightly higher pressure.

Notice the added 'red-oxide' primer in the midst of the paint chips on the A6M5b Zero. The primer was added years after the model was built to help make it a bit more accurate. An actual operational Zero, even those that worked in the spartan conditions of Rabaul and the Solomon Islands, would probably not have been this chipped due to the presence of primer. Also note the incorrect colour of the turtle decking behind the pilot's head, which should be a blue-black colour similar to the cowling.

Subtle pre- and post-shading really bring the model to life. It is important when weathering the surface of a model to weather the decals as well. Remember the cardinal rule – 'less is more'!

A6M2 Zero (1/72)

Subject:	*A6M2 Zero*
Modeller/photos:	*Derek Brown/Brian Criner*
Base kit:	*Hasegawa*
Scale:	*1/72*
Additional detailing:	*Scratchbuilding*

This is the 'first generation' A6M2 Zero kit by Hasegawa. The kit was manufactured in the early 1970s and included the ubiquitous boilerplate rivets and raised panel lines. At the time that this model was built (1989) the only 1/72-scale kits available to the modeller were the Frog, Jo-Han and Hasegawa offerings, with the Hasegawa being the best of the three.

I wanted to improve on the basics that the kit offered, and began by completely scratchbuilding the interior, landing gear, wheel wells and engine. This model

This is the old-tooled version (1970s) of the Hasegawa A6M2 Zero, painted in the markings of Saburo Sakai's aircraft in which he was nearly shot down by an SBD Dauntless rear gunner over Guadalcanal in 1942. The original kit had raised panel lines and lacked detail compared with the re-tooled Hasegawa kit available today.

The model was super-detailed by scribing panel lines, and adding a complete cockpit, a scratchbuilt engine, vacuformed canopy and cowling, dropped flaps, folded wing tips, scratchbuilt landing gear and fuselage improvements like a step, landing gear indicators, a tailhook, and formation lights. Derek completely scratchbuilt the Sakae 12 radial engine.

The scratchbuilt landing gear includes solder for brake lines and sections of stainless steel tubing sleeved into the slightly larger diameter tubing for the oleo strut. Saburo Sakai flew with the Tainan Air Corps, which decorated the aircraft with the blue band. Current research seems to indicate that red and yellow bands were also used, so check your references for the latest theories on markings. Also notice the cut-down radio mast. Since the radios in the early Japanese Zero was not very effective, they were often removed and the mast chopped down to the canopy to save weight and reduce drag on the airframe.

was built prior to the emergence of aftermarket products, so all that you see was constructed using plastic card, brass tubing (for the landing gear) and fine-gauge wire. References used were the wonderful *Maru Mechanic* book, the Monogram *Japanese Interiors* book and photos of real Zeros that I took at museums.

I wanted to showcase on this model a technique for building an engine out of punched discs, and figured a scratchbuilt Sakae 12 engine in 1/72 scale would do the trick. I used a Waldron set to punch out nearly 500 small discs from .005-inch sheet plastic, and 'stacked' the discs by alternating the cooling fins with smaller diameter spacers to achieve the cylinder effect. A scratchbuilt firewall, exhaust system, oil tank and cowling flaps completed the 'exposed' look.

The control surfaces were repositioned, panel lines were scribed and the model painted with Gunze and Tamiya acrylics. Even though today's advancements in resin aftermarket products and pre-painted photoetch make detailing interiors much easier, you can still do it the 'old school' way and produce a very detailed model.

A close up of the 1/72-scale scratchbuilt A6M2 engine for Saburo Sakai's aircraft.

A6M2b Zero (1/144)

Subject:	*Zero*
Modeller/photos:	*Brian Criner*
Base kit:	*Sweet Aviation Models*
Scale:	*1/144*

A good friend sent me the Sweet 1/144-scale kit as a gift and joked 'I bet you could build it in a day'. Looking at the kit, I thought, 'That's a great goal'. Thus I proceeded on my 'Zero in a day' project. The kit comes with enough sprues to produce two Zeros as well as a variety of different decaling schemes. Sure enough, I was able to build almost all of the kit in a day. Interestingly, it took nearly as long to mask the canopy as it did to build the rest of the kit. Built up, and with a bit of weathering, the kit is a nice representation of the Zero.

The Sweet kit is really 'sweet'. It comes with sprues to build two complete aircraft as well as a variety of decaling schemes. Panel lines are very subtly done and the shape of the model looks, well, like a Zero!

ABOVE The decals for the prop are incredibly small and a real challenge to line up properly. There are no holes or indents to represent the gun ports. Unfortunately, in my haste, I forgot to open them up.

BELOW The Sweet kit is a wonderful piece of engineering that can be made into a convincing representation of the Zero.

Cockpit detailing for an A6M3 Zero (1/48)

Subject:	*Cockpit detailing for an A6M3 Zero*
Modeller/photos:	*Derek Brown*
Base kit:	*Hasegawa A6M3-32*
Scale:	*1/48*

Derek Brown is one of the world's great modellers. His attention to detail is amazing. He has won several first-place and grand prize trophies at the IPMS US nationals and has had his work published in magazines such as *Fine Scale Modeler*, *AFV* and *Tamiya Model Magazine*. It just so happens Derek is a die-hard fan of the Zero, and is also the official photographer for the rebuild of an A6M3 to flying condition by Vintage Aircraft Ltd. in Ft Collins, Colorado. When I asked Derek if he would be willing to build a Zero for this book he almost fainted.

Derek was unable to finish the build in time for the book, but I really wanted to share his amazing detailing work on the cockpit with readers. Derek's house has recently gone through a major renovation, which includes a new model room for his creations. When he finally gets back to modelling, he has promised to finish the model in the same markings as the Evergreen Zero and offer it as a gift. What a guy!

The areas in and behind the cockpit were painted black in order to eliminate the need to carry the detail further into those areas. When one views the details from the closed cockpit this gives the illusion that the detail carries further into the aircraft.

Derek has detailed the interior of the Zero using a combination of plastic, resin aftermarket sets, and photoetch. The area behind the seat was detailed by adding oxygen bottles and CO_2 bottles for charging the Zero's weapons.

The detailing on the starboard side of the cockpit.

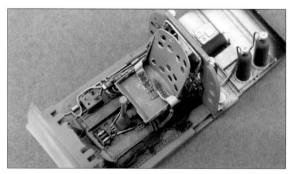

A shot of the cockpit floor from above. The seatbelts are the pre-painted versions from Eduard. The ability to pre-paint photoetch has added incredible details to these parts (notice the stitching) but also brings some challenges when trying to match the colours of such items as the pre-painted instrument panel.

References and further reading

Anderton, David, *Aggressors: Interceptor vs. Heavy Bomber*, Howell Press, 1991.

Bueschel, Richard M., *Mitsubishi A6M1/2/-2N Zero-Sen: In Japanese Naval Air Service*, Schiffer Military, 1995.

Bueschel, Richard M., *Model Art #272 – Camoflauge and Markings of the Imperial Japanese Navy Fighters in WW II*, Model Art Co. Ltd.

Bueschel, Richard M., *Model Art #323 – The Type Zero Carrier Fighter*, Model Art, Co. Ltd.

Brown, David, *Kamikaze*, Gallery Books, 1990.

Brown, David, *Koku-Fan #3*, Bunrin-Do, Co., 1977.

Campbell, Christy, *Air War Pacific: The Fight For Supremacy In the Far East: 1937 to 1945*, Crescent, 1990.

Horikoshi, Jiro, *Eagles of Mitsubishi: The Story of the Zero Fighter*, Washington, 1970.

Horikoshi, Jiro, *Famous Airplanes of the World #5 – Type Zero Carrier Fighter Model 11-21*, Bunrin-Do Co., 1987.

Horikoshi, Jiro, *Famous Airplanes of the World #9 – Type Zero Carrier Fighter Model 22-63*, Bunrin-Do Co., 1988.

Horikoshi, Jiro, *Famous Airplanes of the World #56 – Type Zero Carrier Fighter Model 22-63*, Bunrin-Do Co., 1996.

Janowiez, Krzysztof, *A6M2-N Rufe*, Kagero, 2004.

Juszczak, Artur, *Mitsubishi A6M Zero*, Mushroom Model Publications #6103, 2001.

Masahiko, Takeda (Ed), *Koku-Fan #53 – A6M Zero Fighter*, Bunrin-Do Co., 1990.

Mikesh, Robert C., *Japanese Aircraft Equipment*, Schiffer Military, 2004.

Mikesh, Robert C., *Japanese Aircraft Interiors: 1940–1945*, Monogram, 2000.

Mikesh, Robert C., *Zero: Combat & Development/History of Japan's Legendary Mitsubishi A6M Zero Fighter*, Motorbooks, 1994.

Mikesh, Robert C. and Watanabe, Rikyu, *Zero Fighter*, Zokeisha Publications, 1981.

Mikesh, Robert C. and Watanabe, Rikyu, *Zero Fighter Watching*, Kojinsha Co., 2005.

Nohara, Shigeru, *A6M Zero in Action*, Squadron/Signal, 1983.

Nohara, Shigeru, *Aero Detail #7: Mitsubishi A6M Zero Fighter*, Dai Nippon Kaiga Co., 1993.

Pajdosz, Waldemar and Zbiegniewski, Andre R., *3/202 Kokutai*, Kagero, 2003.

Preston, Anthony, *Decisive Battles of the Pacific War*, Chartwell Books, 1979.

Sakaida, Henry, *Imperial Japanese Navy Aces: 1937–1945*, Osprey Publishing,1998.

Willmott, H.P., *Zero: A6M*, Chartwell Books, 1980.

Zero colour matrix chart

This chart is intended to help you select the right colours when painting your Zero.

	FS equivalent (or close match)	Model Master Enamel	Tamiya	Gunze	Polly Scale	White Ensign
Mitsubishi						
A6M2 overall *ameiro/hairyokushoku* colour	FS 24201	(1792) SAC Bomber Tan	Exterior colour = 80% (X-2) White + 13% (X-9) Gloss Brown + 4% (X-5) Gloss Green + 1% (X-1) Gloss Black + 2% (X-8) Lemon Yellow	(H-70) RLM 02	(5230) USSR Topside Green	(ACJ07) Mitsubishi Grey
A6M2 control surfaces		66% (1792) SAC Bomber Tan (spray can) + 34% (1745) White	75% Exterior Colour + 25% (X-2) Gloss White	75% (H-70) RLM 02 +25% (H-1) Gloss White	75% (5230) USSR Topside Green + 25% (5011) White	(ACJ07) Mitsubishi Grey
A6M3 overall colour	FS 24201	(1792) SAC Bomber Tan	Exterior colour	(H-70) RLM 02	(5230) USSR Topside Green	
A6M5 upper colour	FS 34052	(2116) IJN Green	(XF-11) IJN Green	(H-59) IJN Green	(5278) IJN Green	(ACJ06) Mitsubishi Green
A6M5 lower colour	FS 34201	(1792) SAC Bomber Tan	Exterior colour	(H-70) RLM 02	(5230) USSR Topside Green	(ACJ07) Mitsubishi Grey
Interior colour	FS 24257 FS 24098	(1715) Interior Green	(XF-71) Cockpit Green	(H-58) Interior Green	(5272) IJA Green	
Engine cowling, deck area under canopy	Blue-Black	30% (1717) Dk Sea Blue + 70% (1747) Gloss Black	30% (X-3) Gloss Royal Blue + 70% (X-1) Gloss Black	30% (X-55) Midnight Blue + 70% (H-2) Gloss Black	30% (5092) Sea Blue + 70% (5214) Night Black	(ACJ08) IJN Navy Cowling
Wheel well colour (all variants)	FS 24201	(1792) SAC Bomber Tan	Exterior colour	(H-70) RLM 02	(5230) USSR Topside Green	(ACJ07) Mitsubishi Grey
Interior of inner gear door covers	FS 24201	(1792) SAC Bomber Tan	Exterior colour	(H-70) RLM 02	(5230) USSR Topside Green	(ACJ07) Mitsubishi Grey
Landing gear strut	FS 17038	(1747) Gloss Black	(X-1) Gloss Black	(H-2) Gloss Black	(5214) Night Black	
Torque links, wheel hub	Fs 320061 Silver over Red Primer	(1781) Silver over (1785) Rust	(XF-16) Silver over (XF-7) Red Primer	(H-8) Silver over (H-13) Red Primer	Silver over (5020) Red Primer	
Inner covers retraction arm	FS 24201	(1792) SAC Bomber Tan	Exterior colour	(H-70) RLM 02	(5230) USSR Topside Green	(ACJ07) Mitsubishi Grey

Flap interior	*aotake*[1]	Clear Blue over (1781) Silver	(X-23) Clear Blue over (XF-16) Silver	(H-93) Clear Blue over (H-8) Silver		(ACJ15) *aotake*
Wooden bumper centre LG covers	FS 37038	(1749) Flat Black	(XF-1) Flat Black	(H-12) Flat Black	(5204) Grimy Black	
U-shaped LG cover linkage	FS 17038	(1747) Gloss Black	(X-1) Gloss Black	(H-2) Gloss Black	(5214) Night Black	
Prop spinner (aluminium finish)	FS 320061 Silver over Red Primer	(1781) Silver over (1785) Rust	(XF-16) Silver over (XF-7) Red Primer	(H-8) Silver over (H-13) Red Primer	Silver over (5020) Red Primer	
Natural metal finish – prop rear side	FS 320061	(1781) Silver	(XF-9) Hull Red		(5366) US Earth Red	(ACJ13) Red Brown
Prop spinner and blades (red-brown finish)	FS 320111	(1785) Rust	(XF-9) Hull Red		(5366) US Earth Red	(ACJ13) Red Brown
Hinomaru red	FS 21136	(1705) Insignia Red	(X-7) Gloss Red	(H-3) Gloss Red	(5020) Red	
Leading edge wing IFF yellow	FS 23538	(1708) Insignia Yellow	(X-3) Goss Yellow	(H-4) Gloss Yellow	(5282) IJN Deep Yellow	(ACUS11) ID Yellow
Engine nose case, accessory gear case	FS 26473	(1721) Medium Grey	(XF-20) Flat Medium Grey	(H-335) Medium Sea Grey	(5258) Medium Sea Grey	(ACJ11) Light Grey
Engine cylinders, magnetos, pumps	FS 17038	(1747) Gloss Black	(X-1) Gloss Black	(H-2) Gloss Black	(5214) Night Black	

Nakajima

A6M2 overall colour	FS 26350	(1792) SAC Bomber Tan	Exterior Colour= 80% (X-2) White + 13% (X-9) Gloss Brown + 4% (X-5) Gloss Green + 1% (X-1) Gloss Black + 2% (X-8) Lemon Yellow	(H-70) RLM 02	50% (5230) USSR Topside Green + (5210) 50% Concrete	(ACJ17) Nakajima IJN Grey
	FS 26160				80% USSR Topside Green+ 20% IJA Brown	
A6M Rufe overall colour	FS 26350 to FS 26160				50% (5230) USSR Topside Green + (5210) 50% Concrete	(ACJ17) Nakajima IJN Grey
A6M Rufe flap interior	FS 320061 Silver over Red Primer	(1781) Silver over (1785) Rust	(XF-16) Silver over (XF-7) Red Primer	(H-8) Silver over (H-13) Red Primer	Silver over (5020) Red Primer	
A6M5 upper colour	FS 34077	(2116) IJN Green	(XF-11) IJN Green	(H-59) IJN Green	(5278) IJN Green	(ACJ03) Nakajima IJN Green
A6M5 lower colour	FS 36350	(1792) SAC Bomber Tan	Exterior colour	(H-70) RLM 02	50% (5230) USSR Topside Green + (5210) 50% Concrete	(ACJ17) Nakajima IJN Grey
Fabric control surfaces	FS 26314					
Interior colour (A6M2)	FS 24373 or 24098					(ACJ004) Nakajima Interior

Interior colour	FS 24255					(ACJ004) Nakajima Interior (A6M5)
Engine cowling, deck area under canopy	FS 37038	(1749) Flat Black	(XF-1) Flat Black	(H-12) Flat Black	(5204) Grimy Black	
Wheel well colour (all variants)	aotake [1]	Clear Blue over (1781) Silver	(X-23) Clear Blue over (XF-16) Silver [1]	(H-93) Clear Blue over (H-8) Silver		(ACJ15) aotake
Interior of inner gear door covers	aotake [1]	Clear Blue over (1781) Silver	(X-23) Clear Blue over (XF-16) Silver [1]	(H-93) Clear Blue over (H-8) Silver		(ACJ15) aotake
Landing gear strut	FS 17038	(1747) Gloss Black	Gloss Black	(H-2) Gloss Black	(5214) Night Black	
Torque links, wheel hub	FS 320061 Silver over Red Primer	(1781) Silver over (1785) Rust	(XF-16) Silver over (XF-7) Red Primer	(H-8) Silver over (H-13) Red Primer	Silver over (5020) Red Primer	
Inner covers retraction arm	aotake [1]	Clear Blue over (1781) Silver	(X-23) Clear Blue over (XF-16) Silver [1]	(H-93) Clear Blue over (H-8) Silver		(ACJ15) aotake
Flap interior	aotake [1]	Clear Blue over (1781) Silver	(X-23) Clear Blue over (XF-16) Silver [1]	(H-93) Clear Blue over (H-8) Silver		(ACJ15) aotake
Wooden bumper centre LG covers	FS 37038	(1749) Flat Black	(XF-1) Flat Black	(H-12) Flat Black	(5204) Grimy Black	
U-shaped LG cover linkage	FS 17038	(1747) Gloss Black	(X-1) Gloss Black	(H-2) Gloss Black	(5214) Night Black	
Prop spinner (aluminium finish)	Fs 320061 Silver over Red Primer	(1781) Silver over (1785) Rust	(XF-16) Silver over (XF-7) Red Primer	(H-8) Silver over (H-13) Red Primer	Silver over (5020) Red Primer	
Natural metal finish – prop rear side	FS 320061	(1781) Silver	(XF-16) Silver	(H-8) Silver		
Prop spinner and blades (red-brown finish)	FS 320111	(1785) Rust	(XF-9) Hull Red		(5200) Rust	
Hinomaru red	FS 21136	(1705) Insignia Red	(X-7) Gloss Red	(H-3) Gloss Red	(5020) Red	
Leading edge wing IFF yellow	FS 23538	(1708) Insignia Yellow	(X-3) Gloss Yellow	(H-4) Gloss Yellow	(5282) IJN Deep Yellow	(ACUS11) ID Yellow
Engine cylinders, magnetos, pumps	Gloss Black	(1747) Gloss Black	(X-1) Gloss Black	(H-2) Gloss Black	(5214) Night Black	

[1] Greg Springer has experimented with the illusive aotake colour and has come up with a technique that represents this colour very well. Spray the area silver and let it dry. Mix up various shades of Clear Blue and Clear Green. (Tamiya makes a Clear Blue X-23 and Clear Green X-25 in the acrylic paints.) Since they are quite vivid in tone, the secret to making them accurately resemble aotake is to add a colour called 'Smoke' (X-19 in Tamiya colours), a translucent dark grey. When Smoke is added, the chroma of the blue and especially the green is lessened to a realistic level. Spray the area with the Clear Blue and Green. Alternating colours and how much is applied (multiple mist coats) will provide a variety of shades, which will match the actual appearance of the aotake. Areas prone to heat will tend to have more of a blue tone. Gunze also makes these three colours in their aqueous Hobby Color line.

Zero walkaround

The wheel well of the A6M3 in Chino. The *aotake* is not the original paint and seems too blue. Besides the details of the linkage and plumbing, the exhaust and oil staining around the well are also of interest.

Also, note the wear pattern on the retraction strut of the 'green' well. The wear is from the tiny wheel on the bottom of the gear strut. (GC)

Outboard portion of gear well.

RIGHT The structure just below the tie-down is a wheel that rolls up inside the wheel well. (GC)

BEIOW LEFT Details of the gear.

BELOW RIGHT Cowl flap details on the Chino Zero. (GC)

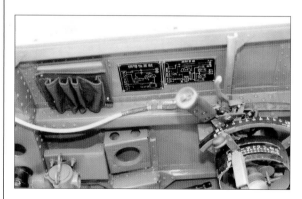

A nice shot of the port side cockpit wall showing the elevator trim wheel, throttle, prop and mixture controls and the flare pocket. (GC)

Close up of the bomb release levers, and trim wheel. The small, butterfly shaped knobs are fuel selector switches. (GC)

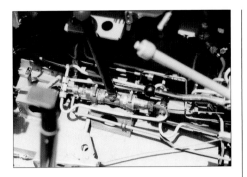

ABOVE Details of the maze of wiring occupying the lower right portion of the cockpit. (GC)

LEFT, TOP Another shot of the wiring occupying the lower right portion of the cockpit. (GC)

LEFT, MIDDLE Seat details on the Ft Collins Zero. (DB)

LEFT, BOTTOM A nice shot of the *aotake* coating on the inside of a wing panel on the Ft Collins Zero. (DB)

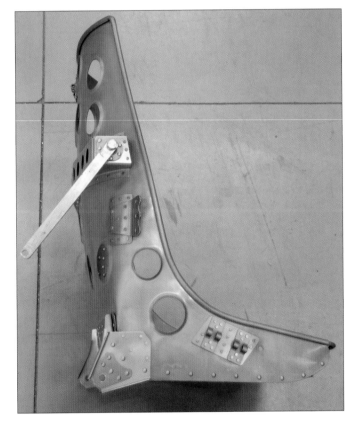

BELOW Details of the area behind the bulkhead on the right side of the cockpit. (GC)

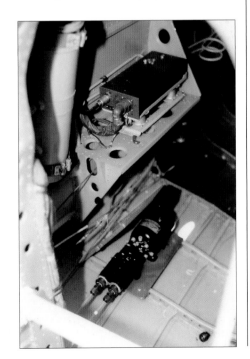

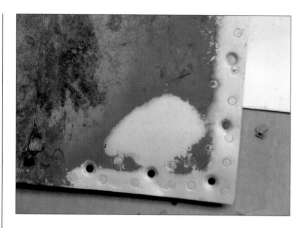

A wheel well panel showing the wearing away of the surface paint down to the metal. (DB)

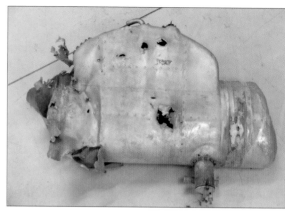

The original oil tank (found just forward of the firewall) from the Ft Collins Zero. (DB)

Canopy latch details. (DB)

A nice shot of the Chino A6M3 showing open hatches and sporting a natural metal finish.

ABOVE Flap details on an A6M2 at the Santa Monica Air Museum. (GC)

ABOVE RIGHT Details of the aileron actuator mechanism on the Chino Zero.

RIGHT Details of the tail wheel from the Chino Zero.

BELOW LEFT More details of the aileron actuator mechanism on the Chino Zero.

BELOW RIGHT Wing details from the Chino Zero. Of interest are the various shades of natural metal finish on the wing.

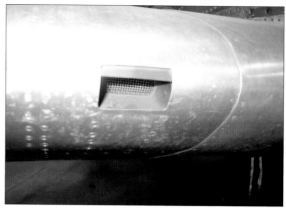

Wing details from the Chino Zero.

Wing details from the Chino Zero.

A shot of a decaying Zero before recovery. Note the red-oxide primer still covers much of the fuselage. (DB)

An interesting discovery made while visiting the Vintage Aircraft Ltd. restoration shop was the presence of a yellow strip just aft of the tailhook well on several derelict fuselage pieces lying around the shop. (DB)

Kits and accessories available

Zero kits

Manufacturer	Description	Scale	Model no.
Minicraft	A6M2 type 11	1/144	MMI14416
Sweet	A6M2b	1/144	
Sweet	A6M2-N Rufe	1/144	
Sweet	A6M2b (green)	1/144	
A+V from Czech	A6M1	1/72	ALV0102
Arii	A6M2-N Rufe	1/72	AR53004
Arii	A6M2 type 21	1/72	AR53005
Arii	A6M5 type 52	1/72	AR53006
Academy	A6M5c type 52	1/72	MH2176
AML from Czech	A6M2-K type 0	1/72	AM72004
Hasegawa	A6M5c type 52	1/72	HE00628
Hasegawa	A6M2b	1/72	HE00666
Hasegawa	A6M5c type 52 Hei	1/72	HE00453
Hasegawa	A6M2-N Rufe	1/72	HE00630
Hasegawa	A6M3 type 22	1/72	HE00377
Hasegawa	A6M2 type 21	1/72	HE00451
Hasegawa	A6M5 type 52	1/72	HE00452
Hasegawa	A6M5c type 52	1/72	HE00453
Hasegawa	A6M2b type 21	1/72	HE00616
Hasegawa	A6M5 type 52	1/72	HE03016
Hasegawa	A6M5 type 52	1/72	HE51322
Testors	A6M5c type 52	1/72	TE861004
Arii	A6M5c type 52	1/48	AR321
Hasegawa	A6M2 type 11	1/48	HE09142
Hasegawa	A6M2 type 21	1/48	HE09143
Hasegawa	A6M2 type 21	1/48	HE09394
Hasegawa	A6M5c type 52	1/48	HE09460
Hasegawa	A6M3 type 22	1/48	HE09495
Hasegawa	A6M3 type 32	1/48	HE09565
Hasegawa	A6M5 type 52	1/48	HE09543
Hasegawa	A6M2b type 21	1/48	HE09573
Hasegawa	A6M5c Samurai	1/48	HE09606
Hasegawa	A6M2b type 21 w/bombs	1/48	HE09626
Hasegawa	A6M2-N Rufe	1/48	HE09069
Hasegawa	A6M5c type 52	1/48	HE09070
Hasegawa	A6M2-N Rufe	1/48	HE09322
Hasegawa	A6M5b OTSU	1/48	HE09428
Hasegawa	A6M5 type 52	1/48	HE09517
Hasegawa	A6M2b type 21	1/48	HE09528
Hasegawa	A6M5 type 52/US markings	1/48	HE51510
Hasegawa	A6M5 type 52 'skeleton'	1/48	HE51940
Nichimo	A6M5 type 52	1/48	NI4806
Revell/Mono	A6M5 type 52	1/48	RMX5222
Tamiya	A6M2 type 21	1/48	TM61016
Tamiya	A6M2-N Rufe	1/48	TM61017

Tamiya	A6M3 type 32	1/48	TM61025
Tamiya	A6M2 type 21 prop action	1/48	TM61509
Tamiya	A6M5c type 52 Hei	1/48	TM61027
Tamiya	A6M2-N Rufe prop action	1/48	TM61506
Nichimo	A6M5 type 52	1/35	NIS3501
Hasegawa	A6M5c type 52	1/32	HE08054
Hasegawa	A6M5c type 52	1/32	HE08146
Tamiya	A6M5 type 52 w/sound	1/32	TM60311
Tamiya	A6M5 type 52	1/32	TM60309
Bandai	A6M5c type 52 Hei	1/24	BA34043
Trumpeter	A6M2-N Rufe	1/24	TR24410
Trumpeter	A6M2b	1/24	TR24405

Zero parts and accessories

Scale	Manufacturer	Part no.	Description
1/24	Hobby Decal	ST2401 IVI	Dry Transfer Decals Zero Stencils
1/24	True Details	TD 24001	A6M Zero weighted wheels
1/32	Czech Master Kits	5001	A6M5 Zero Exterior Set Landing Gear, Fuel Cells wheel wells for Tamiya
1/32	Czech Master Kits	5002	A6M5 Zero Exterior Set Flaps, Exhaust Pipes, Crank Case, Cylinders, Seat for Tamiya
1/32	Czech Master Kits	5003	A6M5 Zero Armament Set Wing Ammo Covers, Wing and Fuselage Racks for Bombs for Tamiya
1/48	Cutting Edge	48238	Mitsubishi A6M Zero Ailerons Resin
1/32	Eagle Strike	32025	A6M2 Zero Decals for 3 AC 12 NAG, X-1008 Group, 3 NAG Taiwan
1/32	Eduard	XL509	Zero Insignia for Tamiya
1/32	Eduard	JX001	A6M5 Zero Canopy mask for Tamiya
1/32	Eduard	XL024	6M5 Zero Canopy Mask for Tamiya
1/32	Eduard	XL 015	A6M5c Zero Paint Mask Canopy Wheels for Hasegawa
1/32	Eduard	3001	Photo Etch Painted Zero inst panel A6M5 for Tamiya
1/32	Eduard	32064	Photo Etch Zero Interior Superset A6M5 for Tamiya
1/32	Eduard	32065	Photo Etch Zero Exterior Superset A6M5 for Tamiya
1/32	Eduard	32066	Photo Etch Zero Engine Superset A6M5 for Tamiya
1/32	Eduard	3205	Photo Etch Big Ed Set (Interior, Exterior, engine, Paint masks) for TAM
1/32	Eduard	32018	A6M Zero Photo Etch for Hasegawa
1/32	Hobby Decal	ST3201 IVI	Dry Transfer Decals Zero Stencils
1/32	MOSKIT	32-08	Zero Exhaust Mitsubishi A6M5-8
1/32	Pascal Huget		A6M2 Zero Resin Interior (sides, seat, floor, cowl, MGs, magazines) for Tomy/Doyusha
1/48	Czech Master Kits	4120	A6M2/A6M5 Zero Resin Detail Set for Hasegawa kits
1/48	Czech Master Kits	4119	A6M2/A6M3 Zero Sakae Engine Prop and mount exhaust details Resin for Hasegawa
1/48	Czech Master Kits	4131	A6M5/A6M5c Zero Sakae 21 Engine Prop Resin for Hasegawa
1/48	Czech Master Kits	4132	A6M5/A6M5c Zero Interior Set Resin for Hasegawa
1/48	Eagle Strike	48111	Zero Decals Pearl Harbor AC Pt 4 KAGA
1/48	Eagle Strike	48109	Zero Decals Pearl Harbor AC Pt 3 SHOKAKU
1/48	Eduard	48306	Photo Etch A6M2 type 21 Hasegawa kits
1/48	Eduard	48314	Photo Etch A6M5 Hasegawa Kits
1/48	Eduard	FE127	Photo Etch A6M5 Hasegawa Kits
1/48	Eduard	XF520	Paint Masks Zero Late National Insignia
1/48	Eduard	EX062	Paint Masks A6M2 Zero/Rufe Canopy Hasegawa
1/48	Eduard	XF145	A6M5 Zero Paint Mask Canopy and Wheels for Hasegawa
1/48	Eduard	EX040	A6M5 Zero paint Mask Canopy Wheels or Hasegawa
1/48	Eduard	48299	A6M2 Rufe Photo Etch for Hasegawa
1/48	Eduard	49217	Z6M5 Pre Painted Photo Etch (Interior, Flaps, Land Gear) for Hasegawa
1/48	Eduard	48121	Photo Etch A6M5 Interior for Tamiya Kit
1/48	Eduard	48122	Photo Etch A6M5 Flaps for Tamiya Kit
1/48	Eduard	48176	Photo Etch A6M3-32 Interior Flaps for Tamiya Kit

1/48	Eduard	49218	A6M3 type 22 Pre Painted Photo Etch for Hasegawa
1/48	Eduard	FE129	A6M2 Zero Photo Etch for Hasegawa
1/48	Eduard	FE218	A6M3 type 22 Zero Pre Painted Photo Etch for Hasegawa
1/48	Eduard	XF519	A6M2 Zero/Rufe National Insignia Paint Mask
1/48	Falcon	3348	Vacuform Canopies (many AC inc Zero)
1/48	Hobby Decal	ST48011V1	Dry Transfer Decals Zero Stencils
1/48	MOSKIT	4834	Zero Exhaust Mitsubishi A6M2 type 21 Nakajima A6m2-N Rufe
1/48	Squadron	9555	Vacuform Canopies for Zero
1/48	Teknics	TK4842	A6M2 Zero Cockpit Superset
1/48	True Details	41010	A6M3/A6M5 x 2 Paint Masks for Hasegawa
1/48	True Details	48005	Zero Resin Weighted Wheels
1/48	Verlinden	1289	A6M2b Zero Type 21 Interior, Details
1/72	A&V Models		Zero Resin A6M1 1st and 2nd prototype resin kits
1/72	AeroMaster	72086	Zero Decals for 6 AC 12th NAG 3rd NAG 582 NAG Tsukuba FG, 203 NAG A6M2-N Rufe 934 NAG
1/72	AeroMaster	SP72-04	Zero Decals – Eagles of the Rising Sun
1/72	AeroMaster	SP72-06	Zero Decals – Special Attack Squadrons
1/72	Aires	7265	A6M2 Zero Resin Cockpit for Hasegawa
1/72	Aires	7019	A6M5 Zero Resin Cockpit for Hasegawa
1/72	Aires	7065	A6M5 Zero Resin Cockpit for Hasegawa
1/72	Airwaves	AC72149	Zero Cockpit Seat and Components
1/72	BMW	0572	Zero Instrument Panel Decals
1/72	BMW	1548	Zero Instrument Panel Decals
1/72	BMW	2532	Zero Instrument Panel Decals
1/72	Czech Master Kits	7009	A6M5c Zero Interior for Academy
1/72	Czech Master Kits	7023	A6M2-K Two Seat Resin Conversion for Academy
1/72	Czech Master Kits	7023	A6M2-K Conversion Set for Hasegawa
1/72	Eduard	73001	Seatbelts – Japanese Army / Navy (color)
1/72	Eduard	XS532	Hinomaru I – Paint Masks
1/72	Eduard	XS 533	Hinomaru II – Paint Masks
1/72	Eduard	CX065	A6M5 Canopy Frames masks for Academy 1/72-scale kits
1/72	Eduard	XS020	A6M5 Paint Masks Canopy for Academy
1/72	Eduard	CX006	A6M5 Paint Mask Canopy for Hasegawa
1/72	Eduard	XS169	A6M5 Zero Paint Masks Canopy and wheels for Hasegawa
1/72	Eduard	72130	A6M3 Zero Photo Etch for Hasegawa
1/72	Eduard	7202	Big Ed Set A6M5c Includes 72384, 73200, XS169, XS522 for Hasegawa
1/72	Eduard	72132	Photo Etch A6M5 for Hasegawa
1/72	Eduard	SS104	A6M5 type 52 Zero Photo Etch for Academy
1/72	Eduard	72283	A6M5c type 52 Interior Photo Etch for Academy
1/72	Eduard	72284	A6M5c type 52 Flaps Photo Etch for Academy
1/72	Eduard	73200	A6M5c Pre Painted Photo Etch for Hasegawa
1/72	Eduard	SS200	A6M5c Zero Pre Painted Photo Etch for Hasegawa
1/72	Falcon	1872	Vacuform Canopies WWII (many AC inc Zero)
1/72	Falcon	2572	Vacuform Canopies WWII (many AC inc Zero)
1/72	Hawkeye Designs	101	Zero Resin Cockpit Set for A6M3 – A6M5 for Hasegawa
1/72	Hobby Decal	ST72011V1	Dry Transfer Decals Zero
1/72	Microscale	72-0068	Decals – Japanese Group Markings
1/72	Microscale	72 0069	Decals – Japanese Group Markings
1/72	Microscale	72-0070	Decals – Japanese Group Markings
1/72	MPD	72602	A6M2 Zero Decals Sakai V-103
1/72	Platz	HD703	A6M2b Decals – 4 AC from 261st NAG
1/72	Platz	HD705	A6M2b Decals – 4 AC from Mariana Fighter Command
1/72	Platz	HD701	Decals for 4 AC - A6M3 Presentation Houkoku AC
1/72	Plus Model	C-056	A6M5 Zero Cockpit Placards (Instruments)
1/72	Tech Mod	72041	A6M2 Zero Decals – 4 AC Tainan Kokutai, Pearl, 170 Konoike Kokutai
1/72	Squadron Signal	9124	A6M Facuform Canopies x 2
1/72	Techmod	72040	Zero Decals for 2 AC 261 Kokutai, P-5016 Chinese National AF

Index

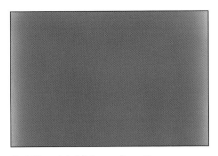

1. Mitsubishi Interior Green

6. *Tsuchi-Iro* **(Grey-Green)**

2. Mitsubishi Cowl Blue-Black

7. Propeller Brown

3. Mitsubishi Navy Green

8. *Aotake* **Preservative**

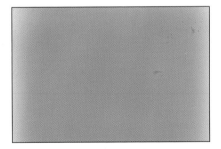

4. Nakajima Interior Grey-Green

9. Slate Grey

5. Red Oxide Primer

6. *Tsuchi-Iro* (Grey-Green)

This was created by Greg Springer by mixing 20 parts SAC Bomber Tan, 11 parts White FS 37875, and 0.9 parts Green Zinc Chromate. It is a controversial colour, previously referred to as *Ame-Iro* and *Hairyokushoku*. Some believe that the light olive colour was due to a lacquer preservative applied over the paint, although this has never been substantiated.

7. Propeller Brown

Found on late model Zeros. The paint is from the Aeromaster enamel line (Red Brown Primer). White Ensign's ACJ13 is a good substitute.

8. *Aotake* Preservative

Start with Testors Buff Silver; cover with Tamiya Clear Blue; then tint with Tamiya Clear Green and a drop of Clear Yellow. This was sprayed on all interior surfaces, but not in the cockpit. Areas that were sealed between two pieces of metal were more blue; those with more air exposure tended to look more green.

9. Slate Grey

This was created by Greg Springer by mixing two parts Dark Slate Grey with one part Flat White. This was the colour of all fabric control surfaces on *Tsuchi-Iro* aircraft. It can be highlighted with Testors Pale Green.

1. Mitsubishi Interior Green

White Ensign Models Colourcoats ACJ18. This is close to American Interior Green. SAC Bomber Green is also a close match.

2. Mitsubishi Cowl Blue-Black

White Ensign Models Colourcoats ACJ08. Used on all Mitsubishi-built Zeros. Nakajima-built Zeros and all Rufes had black-painted cowls, turtle decks, and coamings.

3. Mitsubishi Navy Green

White Ensign Models Colourcoats ACJ06. Initially, all Zeros and Rufes were painted overall *Tsuchi-Iro*. With the need for better defensive schemes, the upper surfaces of most Zeros and Rufes were painted dark green in the field. Eventually, Zeros came from the factory in this scheme.

4. Nakajima Interior Grey-Green

White Ensign Models Colourcoats ACJ04. To be used on all Rufes, and some A6M2s and A6M5s.

5. Red Oxide Primer

Start with a cup of Model Masters Rust and tint to a bloody hue. Colour this with Testors Italian Red. This was reportedly used on all Zeros right up until war's end. This primer made paint peeling less likely.